MAJORITY RULES
COMPLETING THE JOURNEY TO WOMEN'S EQUALITY

LYNN HARDY YEAKEL

Copyright © 2020 by Lynn Hardy Yeakel.

Library of Congress Control Number: 2020901351
ISBN: Hardcover 978-1-7960-8367-5
Softcover 978-1-7960-8366-8
eBook 978-1-7960-8365-1

All rights reserved. No part of this book may be reproduced or transmitted in any form or by any means, electronic or mechanical, including photocopying, recording, or by any information storage and retrieval system, without permission in writing from the copyright owner.

Any people depicted in stock imagery provided by Getty Images are models, and such images are being used for illustrative purposes only. Certain stock imagery © Getty Images.

Print information available on the last page.

Rev. date: 01/27/2020

To order additional copies of this book, contact:
Xlibris
1-888-795-4274
www.Xlibris.com
Orders@Xlibris.com

MAJORITY RULES

CONTENTS

Acknowledgments vii
Dear Reader ix
Introduction xi

SECTION 1. LEARNING FROM THE PAST

Chapter 1 Why the Stories of American Women Matter 1
Chapter 2 Stand Up and Be Heard 8
Chapter 3 I Can Do That! 14
Chapter 4 Somebody Has to Be First 20
Chapter 5 One Vote Can Create a Landslide 27
Chapter 6 Refusing to Settle 35

SECTION 2. ACTING IN THE PRESENT

Chapter 7   Building On What We've Learned 43
Chapter 8   Balance Is Better 49
Chapter 9   Economic Inequity Can Be Fixed 53
Chapter 10 Risk-Taking Is Required 57
Chapter 11 What If All Women Voted? 65
Chapter 12 Enriching the Present 71

SECTION 3. SHAPING THE FUTURE

Chapter 13 Coalitions Are Crucial 77
Chapter 14 What Equality Looks Like 82
Chapter 15 Overcoming Obstacles 89
Chapter 16 Unfinished Business 96
Chapter 17 Rules for the Majority 101

Appendix 109
Letter to Mae Yeakel and Chloe Arias 111
About the Author 115
Index 117

ACKNOWLEDGMENTS

There are several people without whose help this book would not have been possible, especially at this time. Some have asked to remain anonymous, and I will respect that request. But one important individual must be acknowledged.

I've long been a fan of one of the nation's leading editorial cartoonists, Signe Wilkinson, whom I thank for creating this book's cover art. Her humorous mini-collection, "Herstory, 19 Cartoons in Celebration of the 19th Amendment," is a tiny sampling of the hundreds of cartoons she has drawn chronicling the issues that shape women's lives. Thanks to Signe and the women working together who are changing the world.

It's also important to recognize the many individuals and institutions that have made Vision 2020 possible: Drexel University and its College of Medicine, the home of Vision 2020, the donors and sponsors like The Penn Mutual Life Insurance Company who have invested in the project, and of course Vision 2020's Delegates, Allied Organizations, volunteers, and many others across the country who are doing the work that will bring us to the time when We, the People, are **all** equal.

Dear Reader,

When our nation's Founding Fathers wrote the U.S. Constitution in 1787, they had the foresight to include a provision for amending it in case they left anything out, like over half the population!

The inspiration for the essays in Majority Rules is one of the twenty-seven Constitutional Amendments to date, Number 19, and the milestone year of 2020 when that amendment celebrates its one hundredth anniversary. The Nineteenth Amendment, granting American women's voting rights, represents the first important step toward women's equality, a journey that continues today.

Although I grew up in a family where strong women were very much the numerical majority—my mother and father each had four sisters, and all were born before women could vote—it was the outnumbered men who had the power and authority. Although I got an outstanding education in an all-girls school and women's college, I never learned about the history of American women's long struggle for equal rights.

So my purpose in this book is to **honor the past** by shedding light on some of the remarkable women left out of our history books, to **enrich the present** by sharing some observations from my many decades on this planet (more than half of which have been devoted to working for the advancement of women), and to help **shape the future** by framing some goals to complete the unfinished business of women's equality.

I invite you to take the journey with me, looking back on our rich history and taking a glimpse into a bright future.

Lynn Hardy Yeakel

INTRODUCTION

Women are here to stay. By *here*, I mean in corporate boardrooms, in the U.S. Congress, in the president's chair at major universities, and anywhere else where decisions are being made that influence American life.

The problem is that while women have been 52 percent of the population in the United States for a couple of centuries, there are not enough of us in those positions of power. The gender thumb has been on the scales for a long time, and even now, in what we like to call our enlightened era, only a fraction of leadership jobs have yielded to female occupancy.

Majority ought to stand for something. And leadership should be shared.

One of the extraordinary elements of the American experience is that when our country is in trouble, head-to-head with a crisis, someone special—a person with visionary capabilities—steps forward to remind us of what's possible.

In the eighteenth century, when our nation was too young to know what it wanted to be when it grew up, George Washington was there to say, "Follow me."

In the nineteenth Century, when our country was in danger of abandoning the *United* in the United States, Abraham Lincoln was there to point the way to the preservation of the unity we value so highly.

In the twentieth Century, when an economic depression and a world war tested the will of America as never before, Franklin D. Roosevelt was there to remind us of just how good we could be when we were up against the odds.

Now, in the twenty-first Century, when technology has made seven billion people our next-door neighbors, it's time for the voices of leadership to be those of both women and men.

So much of that challenge is about discovering the possibility of change. **Rosa Parks** found unfair seating arrangements and discovered she could change them. **Ann Dunwoody** found there had never been a female four-star general and realized she could be one. **Sonia Sotomayor** observed that no Hispanic woman had ever been named to the Supreme Court and raised her right hand. Women of New Hampshire found that no State Senate had ever featured more women than men, so in 2008, by a count of 13–11, they made it happen. Majority rules.

It-can-be-done examples are sprinkled throughout the history of women. What's missing is a steady rain, an occasional downpour. We are in need of honestly assessing our present and then enriching it to the point where women's achievements are no big thing, just a natural outcome joining our power and our possibilities.

Where we should be starts with a realistic view of where we are now. In the paragraphs ahead, I've described how I believe women are currently performing in key areas of measurement.

Shared Leadership

Sheer numbers demand action to change the leadership disparities: roughly a 75–25 imbalance in the U.S. Congress, a huge 475–25 deficit in the land of Chief Executive Officers in business, and a 230-year exclusion from the Oval Office. America, as grand as it is, will never know how it might have benefitted all those years by opening its leadership doors to women.

The challenge of improving the current situation is formidable. People in power are notoriously stubborn about giving it up. Guardians of the status quo tend to strengthen the walls of the castle and deepen the moat.

But there are many reasons for optimism. More women are running for public office—and getting elected! We are growing in numbers at all levels of government. And in future Novembers, there will be more wins.

We are also seeing some CEOs and Boards of Directors around the country opening more doors for women in business. The change is slow, but it is happening.

Economic Parity

With so much talk about pay equity, women's compensation compared to men's for equivalent jobs continues to be unequal and has remained stalled. Nonetheless, more women are speaking up and bringing attention to the issue—though a great deal of catchup needs to be done.

One area where women continue to suffer a hit is when they interrupt their career paths to provide caregiving to children or aging parents. The absence of legislatively established paid leave and job protection for such circumstances often stops income flow. And the reality has always been that family caregiving is disproportionally the responsibility of the women in the household.

The U.S. trails other nations in giving credit to women for managing homes and raising children. Until such service is valued and recognized in Social Security benefits and retirement plans, many women, with overall greater longevity, will find themselves in a late-in-life economic squeeze.

Economic independence and equitable gender policies are essential to correct this imbalance.

Civic Engagement

This is no longer an elective for women. If we are to have a fifty-fifty influence on the conduct of the culture we inhabit, we must commit to action and involvement.

That means we'll create, write, speak, support, donate, invent, run for office, push our minds to the limit, and rearrange our lives until we get it right. Going to the city council meeting when you'd rather stay home that night, voting in that primary election even though you have other responsibilities that day, speaking out on a neighborhood issue despite the risk of becoming unpopular, simply picking up a piece of trash discarded by someone who didn't care as much about the environment as you do—there are so many avenues of civic engagement or, let's call it, civic activism.

Most of all, we must stay informed. Read. Study. Let's educate ourselves. Poring over details of a tax bill may not have the appeal of a novel, but it's the entry fee we must pay to achieve equality. Remember, if you're not getting smart about what's going on, someone else is, and you may not like what they do with what they learn.

Youth Education: Awareness of Women's History

We may or may not know that **Mary Barra** was the first woman to become CEO of a major automobile manufacturer or that **Michelle Howard** was the first four-star admiral in the U.S. Navy who was female and African American or that **Katie Higgins** was the first woman pilot to join the Blue Angels (the elite Navy precision-flying team) or that **Janet Yellen** was the first woman to head the Federal Reserve.

These and hundreds of other accomplishments by women must be incorporated into the teaching of history in our schools. Begin that at an early age, and young girls—and boys—will grow up understanding that history is eager to be written and opportunity is unlimited.

Anyone within earshot of me every March understands how uncomfortable I am with the designation of a single month as Women's History Month. I accept that such a designation is well-meant, but it has marginalization written all over it. Setting aside 31 days to highlight more than one half of the population does not compensate for unequal treatment during the other 334 days of the year.

To bring balance to the messages of the classroom, to provide a presence for women on our currency and in our museums and monuments, and to end Women's History Month and promote respect all year-round—that's the path I advocate.

Mutual Support

Are some women envious of other women who win promotions? Yes. Instead of celebrating the success as beneficial to all women, some submit to the temptation to resent the moment—and perhaps worry that the quota of women will be taken. Do women prefer to have a man for a boss? Some will say yes. Is there a tendency for some women who have achieved success and reached a position of power to forget where they came from and to join the old boys' club? Why is that?

We count on women leaders to remember that the power of their example is more change-making than the authority of their rank. When more women support one another in their endeavors, more progress is made. Women must respect the fact that by helping one another, we are setting an example for the next generation as well as boosting opportunity for all.

Workplace Respect

Is the quest for equality for women hard work? It is if we do it right.

Mutual respect among women and men in the workplace—and in the home—should be automatic in a perfect world. But until that kind of utopian climate arrives, women must recognize that sexism is not somebody else's problem—it belongs to all of us. Fortunately, abusive treatment of women in the workplace has lately been brought to light, with women refusing to put up with harassment. Still, too many women in too many cases refuse to speak up when bad conduct does take place.

Offensive jokes. Degrading remarks. Inappropriate behavior. Giving them a pass merely invites worse behavior tomorrow. Trained to absorb workplace abuse, women can find it difficult to reverse that orientation. Is it hard work? It is if you do it right.

Timetable

Throughout history, many women have been peculiarly patient about achieving their long-delayed equality. And steps toward progress have often produced a backlash from people in power who have stalled that progress and even set it back. Despite occasional surges of emotion when anger about an insult spurs us to march, shout, or write a letter to the editor, women have demonstrated a complacency about inequality.

That's strange. We are certainly impatient about some things. We're impatient with the driver ahead making a left turn or that idiot behind us honking his horn. We can be impatient with appointments when we are kept waiting. I am personally impatient with procrastinators who don't get the job completed on time. Yet many of us are nonchalant about two-hundred-plus years of being supporting actors. Change is a serious business that requires our attention and action.

Expectations

Our expectations are high. I know. We seek a fifty-fifty balance in the leadership roles of business and government. We expect pay to be equitable and long-term economic security for women to be achieved. We expect the elimination of sexual harassment and abuse and the new day of respect.

So our collective commitment is where it ought to be—way up there. What must kick in now is my long-nurtured guideline: Things must be believed to be seen. If we believe, we will create an America where we, the people, are all equal.

To do that, we should start by learning from the past.

SECTION ONE

Learning From the Past

CHAPTER 1

Why the Stories of American Women Matter

Women's history in America has been an untold story, its heroics ignored. It's time for that to change.

My assigned polling place outside Philadelphia used to be a nineteenth Century building. I was told it had been a link in the Underground Railroad that helped transport escaping slaves to freedom. I couldn't help but imagine the courage of the people on the move, seeking a better life, and those who helped them get there. As I took my Election Day walks to vote, two additional thoughts of the past dominated my mind. Both had to do with gratitude.

I was grateful to my parents who had taught me early and often to respect the right to vote and never take it for granted. In my family, voting was not an option; it was an obligation. To vote is to endorse the belief that the government belongs to its citizens.

The second beneficiaries of my gratitude during those walks were those gallant, committed, and persistent suffragists who kept up the fight for three-quarters of a century to win for women the right to vote through the passage of the Nineteenth Amendment to the Constitution in 1920.

These women have mostly been edited out of history books. The deeds and leadership of some were so visible they could not be ignored—women like **Susan B. Anthony**, whose tenacity was unmatched in achieving the voting rights breakthrough, an accomplishment she did not live to see; like **Elizabeth Cady Stanton**, whose pioneering spirit as far back as 1869 fired up the national suffrage agenda; and like **Alice Paul**, whose militancy in support of the Nineteenth Amendment landed her in jail three times.

Anthony, Stanton, and Paul were grudgingly granted some historical recognition and, in recent times, some well-deserved criticism for their tactics; but hundreds of other women who put their reputations on the line to secure the vote and produce a turning point in the quest for women's equality were overlooked or simply ignored.

Remember the timetable. From the 1848 Women's Rights Convention in Seneca Falls, New York, to the ratification of the Nineteenth Amendment in 1920 spans seventy-two years. (And in a strange coincidence of timing, it was another seventy-two years until the first Year of the Woman in politics in 1992.)

In those early years, women didn't have the vote. They couldn't own property in most places. A career beyond homemaking was relatively unthinkable.

The hill was high, but brave women climbed it and eventually persuaded all-male legislatures to correct the unfairness. To do so, some of these women endured ridicule and humiliation almost daily.

Some examples of the lesser-known, but immensely valuable, suffragists will illustrate the essential characteristics required of women who accepted this mission and who decided that they would not listen to those who said that women should not, could not, and would not participate in public life. Instead, these women went about demonstrating why they should, could, and would.

Abigail Jane Scott Duniway demonstrated *perseverance*. A survivor of an 1852 cross-country wagon-train journey that took the lives of her mother and brother, Abigail settled in Oregon. She ran a business, started a newspaper, and turned a half dozen defeats on women's voting rights into an eventual victory, which she saw from a wheelchair as Oregon wrote women's suffrage into its constitution. Beyond her built-in belief that what she was doing was critical to accomplishing full citizenship for women, Abigail understood the value of communications, of getting the message out repeatedly on the worth of women having access to the ballot. Her reward: Abigail Jane Scott Duniway became the first Oregon woman to register to vote.

Anna Howard Shaw exercised *leadership*. Toughened by a Midwest farm background, Anna took her limited schooling and converted it into a life of service—first in the ministry, then as a medical school graduate, then as a lecturer of national note, particularly on the issue of voting rights for women. She followed Susan B. Anthony and Carrie Chapman Catt into the leadership of the National American Suffrage Association. The path to suffrage became a divided one. Anna Shaw and Alice Paul, allied in the mission, had different strategies and went in different directions. Anna died in 1919, just a year prior to the passage of the Nineteenth Amendment, a cause to which she had dedicated much of her life.

Emily Jane Newell Blair took *action*. Unwilling to sit on the sidelines in 1910 as a contented Missouri homemaker, thirty-three-year-old Emily launched a political-action career that, fourteen years later, resulted in her being the only woman national officer of the Democratic National Committee. She had gained stature with her writings both on women's suffrage and on the potential for women with political power. She helped found the League of Women Voters in 1920, but feeling nonpartisanship was not the most effective way for women to influence political action, she joined the Democrats. Emily Jane Newell Blair organized 2,000 women's clubs for the party. She called for a new kind of feminism, urging qualified women to run for office and all other women to support them.

Marguerite Milton Wells demonstrated *loyalty*. Growing up in the Dakota Territory late in the nineteenth Century and already interested in citizenship at age twelve, Marguerite convinced her father to smuggle her into an all-male political meeting—dressed as a boy. Beginning in 1920, her interest led her to the League of Women Voters, to which she devoted twenty-five years of her talent. Winning some battles, losing some, she became the League's third president. Her focus was on getting more women into high-responsibility jobs and erasing legal barriers that had barred women from professional progress. Marguerite Wells had an unfailing belief in democracy and the certainty that when well-informed, the majority of men and women would make the right choices.

Sara Bard Field was committed to *social change*. One unprecedented deed demonstrated the character of this turn-of-the century suffragist. In 1915, national leader Alice Paul selected Sara Bard Field to deliver a petition to President Woodrow Wilson in support of the Nineteenth Amendment. The trip to Washington, DC, from the West Coast to deliver the document was by automobile. Remember, it was a century ago. There weren't that many cars, and many of the roads that did exist were barely passable. Sara's journey took her to towns along the route where she stopped to gather more signatures. Muddy roads, blizzards, and mechanical breakdowns were a part of the adventure; but the signatures were presented to the President on December 6, 1915.

Lavinia Lloyd Dock had *vision*. She lived for ninety-eight years, and it was said of her that "she used every one of them to advance the independence of women." A feminist by the age of twelve, she trained as a nurse. Upset by the lack of respect nurses received in the workplace, she helped to create the American Nurses Association and influenced nurses everywhere with her stand-on-your-own-feet messages in the *American Journal of Nursing*. Arrested in 1896 in New York for trying to vote, she was released by Police Commissioner Theodore Roosevelt. What followed was a thirteen-day hike to Albany, rallying suffrage support; and later, as a part of Alice Paul's campaign for the vote in Washington, DC, she was jailed three times for picketing in support of the Nineteenth Amendment. She became a leading spokesperson for the 1923 Equal Rights Amendment, repeatedly saying that winning the vote "was only part of the challenge."

If these names aren't familiar, it's because the achievements of women have historically been discounted.

Resistance to change was fierce. Just revisit what the suffragists went through to push the Nineteenth Amendment over the finish line through the following numbers:

> 19—The number of U.S. Congresses that they had to lobby, one after the other

> 480—The number of visits to state legislatures to convince legislators to take up the amendment

> 277—The number of missions to state party conventions just to get the issue in platforms

> 30—The number of attempts to do the same thing with national party platforms

> 47—The number of pleas to include women's right to vote in state constitutions

> 56—The number of votes on the issue, all taken among male voters

In 1917, **Alice Stone Blackwell** compiled for the National Woman Suffrage Publishing Company a list of reasons people used to oppose the Nineteenth Amendment. These objections appeared in editorials, in speeches, and in mailings. Among them are the following:

- Women are already represented by their husbands, fathers, and brothers.

- The bad women would outvote the good ones.
- Men, by nature of their occupations, know more about these things than women, and hence are better fitted to run a city or state.
- The growth of civilization is marked by specialization and division of labor. Women's suffrage would set this back.
- Women would cease to be respected.
- Women are already overburdened.
- It would lead to family quarrels and divorce.
- Women are too emotional and sentimental to be trusted with the ballot.
- We have too many voters already.
- It will turn women into men.

One depressing aspect of those arguments was that a substantial number of women used them to express their opposition to securing the right to vote, which made the work of the suffragists that much harder. While we can't imagine women of today being deprived of the vote, that lack of sisterly support is still evident in other aspects of the unfinished business of women's equality.

If the contributions in many fields by women are not taught, girls and women have only a vague understanding of what—and who—it took to get where we are now. They have a right to know that **Lucy Taylor** earned a dental degree in 1866, defying the odds and overcoming vigorous resistance; that **Mary Harris** was a key figure in organizing labor and standing tall for worker's rights (she would become known as Mother Jones); that **Candy Dykstra** became the first woman to acquire a dealership from the Ford Motor Company; that movie star **Hedy Lamarr** had a brilliant scientific mind that made a major contribution to the U.S. Department of Defense; and, yes, that **Billie Jean King** beat Bobby Riggs at tennis and **Jackie Mitchell** was the first woman to pitch in professional baseball.

On April 2, 1931, in Chattanooga, Tennessee, she struck out Hall of Famer Babe Ruth. You can look it up.

These women, and thousands more like them, each made the case for equality. What's missing is an awareness of all they did. Where are the history books? Where are the monuments? Where are the exhibits?

I think about these women of another time, particularly when I make that trip to vote. The history they created should command our attention so that every new generation of girls starts off hearing about their possibilities, not their limitations. Knowledge of women's history should excite and inspire them about their futures.

CHAPTER 2

Stand Up and Be Heard

> If women are free to pursue excellence, and men are too, we'll not only have positive results but also positive results compounded.

The women we honor as pioneers in the pursuit of equal footing with men understood the ground rules. In their day, men were asked about their work. Women were asked about their husbands and children. Women married early and were taught to think it was the ultimate measure of success.

When women in the nineteenth Century began to become restless about being the caboose on the human train, they quickly discovered that one voice could define the change that was needed but many voices together suddenly improved the hearing of men in power. "Men weren't really the enemy," said feminist **Betty Friedan**. "They were fellow victims suffering from an outmoded masculine mystique that made them feel unnecessarily inadequate when there were no more bears to kill."

Women got organized and raised the volume, and leaders began to emerge—**Elizabeth Cady Stanton**, **Lucretia Mott**, **Sojourner Truth**, and others.

Leadership Firsts

Leaders then and leaders now are essential for changing what is to what can be. Every impassioned cause needs a cool head. Every adventuresome undertaking needs a take-charge advocate. Every small thought needs a mind that will expand it.

Doubt about outcome, fear about consequences, and temptation to give it all up and play it safe—all these circumstances require a voice of reason saying, "Yes, we can do that, and here's how." The worth of studying women's history can be measured by comparing their time to ours. What did they face? How did they handle the difficulties of their day? What can we learn from them?

Barriers were everywhere for women who sought to have unconventional careers. They had to battle for the privilege of using their brains and other skills. In almost every line of work, with the possible exception of nursing or some teaching or secretarial work, the professional door was closed for women.

But trailblazing leader and world-famous writer **Pearl Buck**—who attended my small college in Virginia, Randolph-Macon Woman's College, many years before I did—emerged, initially using a man's name so publishers would not instantly dismiss her manuscripts. She later won the Nobel Prize in Literature while raising eight children, six of them adopted. And **Amelia Earhart's** family objected to her desire to have a career as an aviator. Male pilots discouraged her by telling her flying was a man's job. Find something safe. Become a nurse. So she did become a nurse, just long enough to save money to buy her own airplane. From that point on, she achieved fame, world records, and a place in history.

Lesser known, but just as determined, **Phoebe Fairgrave,** at the age of seventeen, used an inheritance to buy her own plane, then talked a movie studio into letting her do aerial stunts for the film series *Perils of Pauline*. She married a pilot, opened a flying school, and was appointed by President Franklin D. Roosevelt as the first woman to serve as a government aviation official—a position she asked for out of the belief that if you really want to hold a certain job, "you have to let people know you want it."

But not all women immediately rallied to the cause. There was nothing automatic about gaining the support of women for their own rights. Suffragists were met early and often with anger by many women who felt that voting was properly left to men, a point of view they had been conditioned to accept. The elephant in the room was change. Either resigned to or content with a social role inferior to that of men, many chose not to rock the boat in which they were the passengers.

Women's lack of comfort with the Nineteenth Amendment granting their right to vote became evident quickly. In the first twenty years after the amendment was passed in 1920, the women actually voting in an election seldom exceeded 40 percent.

The word that recurs in the examples above is *first*. These women, and many others, carried the burden of being the pioneer in doing what they did. That brings with it a big responsibility. The expectations imbalance sets in, the inevitable conclusion that if a woman should happen to fail, all women, therefore, are incapable of doing the job. Whenever you are the first to do something, expectations escalate, and measurements become unreasonable.

In the twentieth Century, **Barbara Jordan**, the late Congresswoman from Texas, posted a string of firsts in her life of public service. She put the expectations game into perspective: "If you're going to play the game properly, you better understand every rule." In her case, she welcomed the "rule of elevated expectations," feeling that women could improve upon whatever men had achieved in government.

The time is arriving when women in leadership roles are no longer the exception. We will soon see fewer firsts for women.

Overcoming Barriers

From the time **Jeannette Rankin** of Montana became the first woman elected to the U.S. House of Representatives in 1917, women candidates have been on the receiving end of some uneven treatment.

I experienced the double standard in politics firsthand when I ran for the U.S. Senate from Pennsylvania in 1992. Running against longtime incumbent Senator Arlen Specter, I devoted many hours to studying foreign policy and domestic issues. I was well versed in taxes and thoroughly prepared on matters of health care and the economy. On the campaign trail, my opponent talked about economics, the environment, and education. The next day, the newspapers printed his comments on economics, the environment, and education.

I was also making speeches, sometimes at six stops a day, on the topics of economics, the environment, and education. But the next day, I picked up a newspaper only to read about what I was wearing, my haircut, and my voice. I began to understand that comment about Ginger Rogers having to do the same dance steps as the famed Fred Astaire, only she had to do them backward and in high heels. That curious disparity in the treatment of women candidates is less apparent now that there are more of us, but we should all be vigilant in calling it out when it occurs.

Some say men have more experience at leadership than women. Of course they do! But with each woman appointed as a CEO or who gets elected, the strangeness of having a woman in a powerful position will go away.

Brigadier General Wilma Vaught said, "What I wanted to be when I grew up was—in charge."

Differing Strategies

In 1869, when Susan B. Anthony and Elizabeth Cady Stanton formed the National Woman Suffrage Association, it was only a few months before part of the membership broke away to join

Lucy Stone's more conservative American Woman Suffrage Association. That disagreement lasted for twenty-one years until both groups merged into the National American Woman Suffrage Association. The name was longer, but the differences were shortened.

There is nothing in the biological makeup of women that requires us to agree with one another on everything, but the more we can find accord with the big-picture goals, the sooner that elusive aim of equality will be reached.

Suffragists had some lively disputes, some of them with one another, but they found common ground on three matters:

- Life for all women would be better with the right to vote.
- Life for all women would be better with more women in office.
- Life for all women would be better if we were unafraid to speak our minds—at home, in the workplace, and in government halls.

Women's emergence in the world of work outside the home does not diminish the value and importance of the traditional role as CEO of the family. What the women of our history did was illustrate that homemaking and motherhood isn't all we can do.

By studying women's history, we can avoid some obsolete assumptions. I went to an all-girls high school and an all-women's college. Women's history was not included in the curriculum. So when I graduated from college with honors and went with friends to New York City, I thought I would find a good job. For six weeks, I looked. For six weeks, I was interviewed. For six weeks, I was not asked about my academic performance. Instead, I was asked, "Can you type?" My assumptions did not include the reality of discrimination against women. Knowledge of women's history might have helped prepare me to enter the job market.

We can gain a greater appreciation of what our mothers, grandmothers, and great-grandmothers experienced. Where my appreciation flourishes is in reflecting on what they did *without* in managing their family and household responsibilities. Home appliances were limited. No dishwashers. Doing the laundry was a primitive task. The cooking, sewing, keeping the family together, not to mention the absence of birth control—I think of these things whenever I'm tempted to complain about hard work.

The study of women's history is valuable, particularly in understanding the hurdles faced, the ridicules endured, and the rejections overcome, all for the right to be treated as equals.

CHAPTER 3

I Can Do That!

"Just don't give up on trying to do what you really want to do. Where there is love and inspiration, I don't think you can go wrong."

Ella Fitzgerald, The First Lady of Song, said those words. If you want global fame as a unique singer with a career that lasts six decades and music that will endure forever, you must replace your fear with faith and say, as she did at age seventeen, "I can do that!" Historical boundaries between women's and men's roles have resulted in women not doing certain things because we never tried.

When I was growing up, Ella was my favorite singer, and I collected most of her albums—songs by Cole Porter, Rodgers and Hart, and others. Two of my favorite songs were "Love for Sale" and "Let's Do It!" It was not until many years later that I learned Ella Fitzgerald's fascinating story and how she came to "do it." That is, she became one of the most famous singers of the twentieth Century.

In 1934, when Ella's name was pulled in a drawing at Harlem's Apollo Theater, she won the opportunity to compete as a dancer on Amateur Night. She loved dancing. But just before she was due to go on, the act ahead of her featured dancing sisters who, she realized, were a whole league above her.

Giving up her spot on the show was not an option, but there was no way she was going to follow that dancing act with one of her own. She decided to sing instead, which turned out to be a good decision. The audience insisted on an encore, and a sixty-year career began. Ella Fitzgerald's talent became a gift to all because she said "I can do that."

When Vision 2020, a national coalition of individuals and organizations seeking equality for women, was formed in 2008, one part of its triangle of purpose was to "learn from the past," to make sure that the overlooked women achievers of history finally found the spotlight they deserved.

What came out of our early research was a sustained admiration for so many women, including those referenced here, who took the first steps. They went where women had not ventured. In an early American culture dominated by the philosophy that "man makes a house, woman makes a home," the pattern of one's life was pretty clearly defined. In the nineteenth and early twentieth Century, there was little opportunity to find out if a woman's mind could advance science, commerce, or government because her assignment was raising children and supporting her husband.

To visualize something beyond that limited job description—seeing something not yet experienced—a woman had to break out of the mold cast for her by others and do so at the risk of her reputation. To borrow an often quoted phrase, "well-behaved women rarely make history."

So we celebrate some women who have done that. One is **Oveta Culp Hobby**. Born in 1905 in Killeen, Texas, just over a hundred miles south of Dallas, she lived a life in which she never met a challenge she was afraid to take on with confidence in her ability and clarity in her purpose.

Parliamentarian of the Texas House of Representatives; publisher of the *Houston Post*; consultant to the Hoover Commission on governmental efficiency; the first Secretary of the newly created U.S. Department of Health, Education, and Welfare; a director of the Corporation for Public Broadcasting—these were a few of her punctuation marks that may have been overshadowed by a key exclamation point she accomplished during World War II.

With millions of women taking over factory jobs to free up men for military duty, the War Department (now the Department of Defense) saw the need to develop the Women's Auxiliary Army Corps, enlisting thousands of women into the Army to actively fill key jobs that would release men for combat readiness.

The name *Auxiliary* was dropped—an overdue decision given that the dictionary defines it as "acting in a subordinate capacity." Selected to plan, organize, and build the WAC was thirty-seven-year-old Oveta Culp Hobby. At first a Major, then a Colonel, she rallied one hundred thousand women to answer the call, and "women and the military" became a phrase that would never again sound strange.

Finding this in our history books? That's another story, and one for which a happy ending needs to be written. It is invaluable for girls growing up to understand that women ahead of them had the talent and tenacity to prove their worth to the world.

It would be fitting that such an inclusive account of history also features **Mary McLeod Bethune**, who was hailed as "living the most productive eighty years a human being has ever known." She combined her skills as a leader and orator with her dedication to education and civil rights to become one of America's most influential changemakers in the first half of the twentieth Century.

Born in 1875 as the fifteenth of seventeen children of former slaves, she exhibited a lifelong energy devoted to equality for African Americans in an era when no such national commitment existed. Her Bethane-Cookman University has an almost 120-year history, with roots that go back to her opening of a school in a rented house with a student body of five little girls and her own son.

She began that school with $1.50.

Mary Bethune's strength was her powerful personality and unfailing belief that her school could grow. And it did.

To become Daytona Normal and Industrial Institute, training three hundred girls on a twenty-acre campus. The 1923 merger with Cookman Institute created Bethane-Cookman University, now with a modern-day enrollment of four thousand students, women and men.

Her leadership was the natural outcome of her passion for whatever needed to be done. "The drums of Africa still beat in my heart," she said. "They will not let me rest while there is a single Negro boy or girl without a chance to prove their worth."

She posted a stunning list of achievements in education and civil rights activities. Along the way, she became a friend and confidant of First Lady Eleanor Roosevelt and an inexhaustible ambassador of the value of dignity for the individual. She died in 1955 and was buried on the campus of her beloved college.

Oveta Culp Hobby, Mary McLeod Bethune—history has no right to omit such inspirational examples. History's message seems to depend on who's delivering it. To ignore what women did is to deny it.

More girls and women need to know about **Rose Pesotta**, if for no other reason than her story will convey the reality that you don't have to be universally loved to make your mark as a leader. Let's pick up her story from the past in the year 1913. She was seventeen and had already resisted parental pressure to find a man, settle down, and get married. She took a New York job in a shirtwaist factory where she joined the International Ladies' Garment Workers' Union, an association that would continue for a half century.

Rose became so effective at organizing women garment workers that the ILGWU sent her nationwide to conduct unionizing campaigns in some of the hottest anti-union environments of the '20s and '30s. She became the only woman vice president on the union's executive board—an honor for some women, but a cause of outrage for her. In 1942, she refused to run for a fourth term as vice president. She had done the math. Of the union's 305,000 members, 85 percent were women. Still, the union had a policy of having only one woman on its governing board. "Someday," she told them, "I hope the membership will take this so-called rule and throw it out the window." Rose Pesotta returned to her job as a sewing machine operator. Her obituary was carried in the *New York Times* on December 8, 1965. For those compiling "I Can Do That!" rosters, her story should continue.

These three illustrations of women represent a legacy of willingness to try when others wouldn't. They are examples of the kind of human characteristics that worked then and still do now. Hobby's confidence, Bethune's energy, Pesotta's assertiveness—but I must add another to the list that I don't want forgotten. What she exhibited was a competitive spirit that was unsurpassed, and in the career she chose, that spirit was essential.

Althea Gibson's story eliminates any excuses we may have just because people tell us "You can't do that."

You can't possibly go from 143rd Street in Harlem and shake the hand of the Queen of England. You can't possibly become the Jackie Robinson of women's tennis and become the first African American to compete in what is now the U.S. Open. You can't possibly win the 1957 World Championship of Tennis at Wimbledon and return to the U.S. to a ticker-tape parade in New York City twenty-one years after track legend **Jesse Owens** was so honored. And you can't possibly win fifty-six national and international titles while becoming the first American woman of color to appear on the covers of *Sports Illustrated* and *Time* magazines.

All the things Althea Gibson was told she could not do merely served as challenges to be overcome. In her own words, "The loser is always a part of the problem. The winner is always a part of the answer. The loser has an excuse. The winner has a program. The loser says it may be possible, but it's difficult. The winner says it may be difficult, but it's possible."

Quite apart from her tennis accomplishments is an incident that, all by itself, qualifies her as a must-study in women's history. With her fame already established, she was cast in a John Ford movie with heavyweight stars like John Wayne and William Holden. The picture was called *The Horse Soldiers*, a film about the War Between the States. The script called for Althea, who was playing a slave, to speak in stereotypical black dialect. She refused—and won the day by playing the role the way she felt it should be played.

That quality of standing up for what you believe is a characteristic consistently evident in so many women whose courage has advanced the campaign for women's equality.

If no one had taken risks, women would still be seeking the right to vote. If no one had taken risks, women would still be dreaming of becoming doctors, lawyers, engineers, and U.S. Senators. If no one had taken risks, women would still be looking at the limitations, not the possibilities.

At the heart of successful risk-taking is coordination—coordination between high expectations and practical reality, between what's perfect and what's possible, and between what you can do as an individual and what can be accomplished on a larger scale in a cooperative effort with others.

You have to search through history to find women like Hobby, Bethune, Pesotta, Gibson, and so many others in order to assemble the learning moments they left for all of us. When you do that, you'll find they invested very little time in hoping their efforts would be successful.

In April of 2018, I first heard about **Ellen Stofan**. She had just been appointed Director of the Smithsonian's National Air and Space Museum in Washington, DC—another first for women. "It's important to have women in leadership positions," she said, "not just for their skill sets but for the inspiration factor."

She brought over two decades of performance in science and technology to the Smithsonian's doorstep. Still, I can't help feeling that Amelia Earhart and other earlier pioneers of aviation like **Jacqueline Cochran** and **Ruth Nichols** contributed to Ellen Stofan's belief that women could do what so many said they couldn't.

CHAPTER 4

Somebody Has to Be First

For many, the high-water mark of women's progress came in 1920 with passage of the Nineteenth Amendment to the U.S. Constitution, securing the right to vote. Some states weren't that patient. One of them was Wyoming.

A thousand years from now, when American history is more like ancient history, the twentieth Century will still be considered the time when women rejected second-class citizenship.

Women shook off the role of being property and added their skills, values, and perspectives to a society that had generally limited them to supportive roles.

The resistance was stubborn, but decade by decade, women staked claims to the freedoms they had been denied for so long. They forever put aside old expectations of seldom being seen and never heard.

This road of philosophical resolve, educational growth, technological progress, and "I'm not going to take it anymore" grandly opened up for women in August of 1920, in Tennessee, when a young state legislator—with encouragement from his mother—cast the vote that put the Nineteenth Amendment over the top. Enough states, thirty-six, had now ratified the amendment to end a century-and-a-half of neglect.

A spark that had been kindled by **Abigail Adams** late in the 1700s, fanned into flame by Elizabeth Cady Stanton, and set to burning brightly by Susan B. Anthony, put an end to an American embarrassment. Stanton had characterized the ridiculousness of it as early as 1848 at the historic Seneca Falls, New York, Women's Rights Convention. She said, "Drunkards, idiots, horse racing, rum-selling rowdies, ignorant foreigners—all had this privilege denied to women." Elizabeth was not hampered by political correctness in her time.

During the seven decades that followed, the country held its ground that voting was a male-only privilege. Tens of thousands of women became involved, and many were ridiculed by their own families, sometimes jailed and often betrayed by elected officials. When women turned up the heat in their campaign for voting rights, the keep-everything-the-way-it-is crowd produced multiple objections. Women looked for a breakthrough and found it in a place they didn't expect.

Go West

Wyoming is known for its scenic wonders. That's where you'll find the first and probably best-known national park—Yellowstone. You can follow the millions who discover nature's showcase in Jackson Hole. You can satisfy your pioneering quest by visiting Cheyenne Frontier Days. The Grand Teton National Park invites your awe.

When you check where Wyoming stands in population (six hundred thousand total) among the fifty states, you will find it fifty-first, even behind Washington, DC. Yet it was first in granting women the right to vote. That happened in 1869, while the Wyoming Territory was still twenty-one years away from statehood. Wyoming was also the first to elect a woman as Governor. **Nellie Ross** was sworn in on January 5, 1925. And it was first to seat an all-woman jury (1870), to elect a woman as superintendent of public instruction (1894), and to appoint a woman as a justice of the peace.

In every endeavor to bring about change, Wyoming has a history of pioneering, with no apparent problem including women in the voting booth a half century before the right was approved nationally. Some states have elaborate slogans, but Wyoming's is a simple two-word motto: Equal Rights.

Somebody has to be first.

No coverage of Wyoming's leadership in women's rights can omit the story of the life of Governor **Nellie Ross**. History will record that she served as Governor for two years. She graduated from Miltonvale High in 1892, and her family moved to Omaha. Nellie taught kindergarten for four years and gave private piano lessons, but she did not confine herself to the stay-at-home life generally assigned to women at the turn of the twentieth Century. Courtesy of her brothers, she visited Europe.

In 1900, her travels took her to Tennessee, where Nellie Davis Tayloe met Attorney William Ross, who was determined to live and practice law in the West. After their marriage in 1902, when Nellie was twenty-six, they moved to Cheyenne, Wyoming. Twenty years later, William moved to the Governor's office just down the street, but he unexpectedly died after only a year and a half in office. Wyoming law stipulated that his successor must be elected. The Democratic Party quickly nominated Nellie despite her making it clear that she would not campaign because of her responsibilities raising the four Ross sons.

Proud of being the first to grant the vote to women, the citizens of Wyoming seemed eager to be the first to elect a woman Governor. In office, Nellie Ross pushed tax cuts, aid to farmers, and laws that protected women and children. Running for reelection in 1926, she lost narrowly. "I didn't campaign for myself, and I supported prohibition," she said. But win or lose, she did not go quietly into obscurity.

At the Democrat's national convention in 1928, the year Al Smith was nominated for President, Nellie Ross received thirty-one votes from ten states for Vice President on the first ballot. She was promptly named a vice chair of the party's national committee and director of the women's division. In 1933, President Franklin D. Roosevelt called on Nellie Ross to become director of the U.S. Mint, a post she held until 1953, when she retired at the beginning of Dwight Eisenhower's terms as President. The first woman to head up the Mint. Of course. Somebody has to go first, and Nellie Ross was always there to raise her hand.

She spent the final years of her life writing articles for women's publications and traveling the country, making her last trip to Wyoming—to the land of equal rights—when she was ninety-six. She died five years later in Washington D.C., having come a long way from teaching piano lessons.

Keep in mind that the groundwork for her first as a Governor in 1925 was put in place nearly a half century earlier in an unlikely setting. Wyoming was isolated in 1869. Even now, a place like Times Square in New York City regularly draws a million people on New Year's Eve, roughly double the entire population of Wyoming.

So what made Wyoming so visionary in approving suffrage for women?

There are theories that suggest pioneer women were more respected by men because of their strength and endurance in wilderness surroundings. Or maybe it was because women were scarce in the West and men saw the vote as one more way to appeal to them to stay.

Wyoming did not stand alone in granting the vote well ahead of the federal amendment. A year after the 1869 decision there, the Utah Territory also acted. By 1883, the Washington Territory fell in line. When these territories became states, they included women's right to vote in their constitutions.

What was considered a man's world was suddenly more progressive than the eastern states. By 1914, six years before the Nineteenth Amendment finally became law, every state west of the Rocky Mountains already had established women's suffrage. Only Kansas could make that claim east of the Rockies.

How Hard Is It to Go First?

Ask those women who first applied to get into medical school. Ask those women who first entered the boardroom of a Fortune 500 company. Ask jockey **Rosie Napravnik**, the first woman to ride horses in all three Triple Crown races in the same year—Kentucky Derby, Preakness, and Belmont Stakes. Or **Lori Robinson**—that's General Robinson—the first woman to command a major combat unit in the history of the U.S. Armed Forces.

In 1992, I had my own moment of decision. Long before that, my father had alerted me that times would come in my life where the "If not me, who?" question would arise, followed closely by "If not now, when?"

In the previous year, President George H. W. Bush had nominated Clarence Thomas to the Supreme Court. Hearings to examine the nominee's fitness for that position were held by the Senate Judiciary Committee. As a citizen, I watched these televised hearings, never imagining that what happened there was about to change everything I had in mind for the year ahead.

Witnesses for and against the nominee appeared. The questioning was relatively routine, borderline boring. Then Professor **Anita Hill** arrived, bringing charges of sexual harassment against Clarence Thomas, with whom she had worked at the Department of Education and the Equal Employment Opportunity Commission. She reported multiple incidents of misbehavior on his part—episodes he denied.

Quite suddenly, the scene shifted for me and many others. It no longer seemed to be a focus on the nominee's qualifications for the Supreme Court. Now it was a fierce and one-sided contest between this all-male panel and this soft-spoken woman who had been called to testify. The Senators turned their attention to discrediting her and her testimony.

Anita Hill stood her ground. Later, she said, "I think it was the first time that people came to terms with the reality of what it meant to have a Senate made up of ninety-eight men and two women."

The abusive treatment she received during that hearing came in waves. It was a disgraceful display of the misuse of power. One of the most militant Senators on that panel was Pennsylvania's Arlen Specter. His performance, supplemented by others, jump-started the ringing of my phone. On the other end of the line were some very angry women, all united in their belief that a woman had to challenge Specter, who was up for reelection in 1992, and some suggesting that I should be that woman.

Pennsylvania has a population of about twelve million. Slightly over half that number are female. My friends and associates were as fired up as I was that a woman must step up to oppose Specter. I knew several women in the state who might do that. Surely one of them would want to be the first woman from Pennsylvania to be elected to the U.S. Senate.

As time passed, the obvious women decided not to run. I received more phone calls saying, "You must do it." When I decided it was something I wanted to do, I hired a pollster to find the status of my name recognition throughout the state. It turned out to be one percent, but that changed in the next few months as my campaign began. My personal privacy started to evaporate as I set out to raise money, learn the issues, contact the voters, and raise more money.

Winning the five-way Democratic primary was exciting, but the next day, Senator Specter began playing hardball. Politics somehow permits opponents to attack one's family, faith, and point of view. This, I found, was the price for women reaching for equality. On election night, the early results were tantalizingly projecting me as the winner, but as late returns mounted, I realized that wasn't to be.

There is an indescribable emptiness when such a loss follows an entire year of devoting one's energy to a single purpose. It took a while, but later, I understood the importance of what I had done. I found it in the gratitude of women I didn't even know who, to this day, tell me how they supported my campaign and they were inspired by my example. In many ways, that experience was the foundation of my continuing work for women's equality.

From Anita Hill's mention of two women and ninety-eight men in the U.S. Senate in 1992 to the current reality of twenty-five women—one-fourth of the Senate members—we have undeniably made progress, but we'll keep the cork in the champagne bottle until the fifty-fifty mark is reached.

Just because it doesn't always work, it is no reason to avoid trying.

Nearly three decades have passed since my attempt to become the first woman U.S. Senator from Pennsylvania, and still no woman has been elected to this important position.

CHAPTER 5

One Vote Can Create a Landslide

On a day in August of 1920, a single vote brought about a historic change that had been seventy-two years in the making.

Legendary basketball coach **Pat Summitt** had a simple philosophy she shared with her championship teams: "Let's talk about results so we won't have to talk about regrets." In other words: close the deal. It's no surprise that Pat Summitt coached the University of Tennessee women's basketball team to multiple national championships. She was a believer that work and winning were first cousins.

Tennessee has a history of producing winners. Although Tennessee is hailed for its music, so many other women in so many disciplines have brought glory to the land of the Great Smokies, the Grand Ole Opry, Graceland, and dozens of other tourist favorites. Perhaps no woman had a more dramatic moment of influence on history as the lady from Niota.

Niota, Tennessee, is in the southeast part of the state, about fifty miles south of Knoxville and about the same distance north of Chattanooga. In 1920, one of its eight hundred residents was Mrs. J. L. Burn. She was a widow. She owned some land. She had a lot going for her, but as a taxpayer, she was missing one thing—the vote.

The Nineteenth Amendment, approved by the U.S. Congress but still in need of ratification by three-quarters of the state legislatures, came to the table in Tennessee with thirty-five of the thirty-six required states already in the fold. Tennessee's decision would be pivotal. A generous appraisal of the campaign, for and against, would be spirited. A more cynical assessment would include words like *bitter*, *unrestrained*, and *vicious*.

The Lady from Niota

Back in Niota, Mrs. J. T. Burn (her name was **Febb Ensminger Burn**) held a trump card, or so she thought. Her twenty-four-year-old son was in that state legislature in Nashville. In a close vote, she felt she could convince him to vote for ratification despite all the heat faced from the opposition. That heat included heavy persuasion, verbal abuse, and even physical threats.

Some very determined Tennessee suffragists had set the table for this moment. Months, even years, of relentless lobbying were about to get a report card. The strongest support was coming from the area around the city of Memphis and from the Appalachian hill country. It was an unforeseen coalition of big city Democrats and rural Republicans. Strong Tennessee voices for what's right have never been a surprise to me. I know too many personally to underestimate their commitment.

In 2015, our Vision 2020 Delegates and Allied Organizations from all over America convened in Nashville for our fifth National Congress. It was an instantly popular decision, not just because of Nashville's credentials as a great city to visit, but also because it was here that the decisive vote was cast for the Nineteenth Amendment.

Our National Congress coincided with the completion of a monument to the women of the Tennessee suffrage campaign, and I was invited to speak at a reception in the sculptor's studio previewing the monument. As I got ready to speak, I knew my prepared remarks wouldn't do because when I looked at the statue of those five women, I saw something else.

What I saw was my mother and her four sisters—five women who had grown up in Tennessee before the vote, before the first steps toward women's full citizenship the Nineteenth Amendment promised. I thought of them, of how they went to college when most women didn't have that opportunity, and how my mother became a schoolteacher and principal—perhaps not because she wanted to but maybe because the choice of careers for women was so limited.

Yes, I was looking at a statue of five suffragists and thinking about five women in my family, and whatever I said was inspired in part by all ten of those women.

What happened in Tennessee in 1920 was the result of teamwork. The suffragists were organized, capable of lobbying, and unafraid of attempts to belittle their campaign. They were aware and proud of the timetable history had handed them. In 1998, **Carol Lynn Yellin** and **Janann Sherman** put together The Perfect 36, a summary of how the Tennessee vote for the Nineteenth Amendment was achieved. It honors the past in a manner few other documentary pieces can do.

It is my belief that the value of studying the mostly unsung anthem of women's history is not merely to expand one's intellectual storehouse. The worth comes from the blueprint such study inspires for the equality work still waiting for someone to tackle.

Stand Up, Speak Up

The suffragists knew that time, left to itself, could not be trusted. The same mental approach needs to motivate today's women. Time invites us to bend it, shape it, and stretch it—to seize every moment.

No one did that better than Memphis-born **Mary Eliza Church Terrell**. She lived to be ninety and died in 1954 with a reputation for making a difference. "Don't just sit there," her life seems to shout to all of us. "Make something happen that improves the lives of others."

Mary Terrell lived that life during the last half of the nineteenth Century and first half of the twentieth, not a time of robust freedom for women, much less for an African American woman whose mother was a slave.

She was very accomplished and used her time to learn to skate, to swim, to read, to dance, and to ride horseback. She enrolled in Oberlin College in Ohio, refused to take the "ladies' courses," and signed up for classes where she was often the only Black student, sometimes the only woman. She even went to Europe—not to tour ancient ruins, but to become fluent in French, German, and Italian languages.

Everything she did reflected how preciously she regarded time and how devoted she was to others who shared her zeal for independence for the individual. For the young and not-so-young, if they needed someone to inspire them, she was there. For women everywhere, if they needed confidence, she said, "Follow me."

In 1896, the leadership that came naturally to her propelled her, at the age of thirty-three, into the presidency of the National Association of Colored Women, where she served three terms and was made honorary president for life. She lectured, she wrote articles on Black history, and she led delegations to Washington to protest injustice and to seek legislation that would correct it.

She was picketing at the White House when the Nineteenth Amendment was on the line. Always in demand as a speaker, she went to Europe in 1919 to address the Women's International League for Peace and Freedom.

Through the years, she maintained a diary that was even more candid than her book, A Colored Woman in a White World. Her thoughts on women's suffrage were particularly blunt.

> To oppose women's suffrage is the most preposterous and ridiculous thing in the world ... If I were unfortunate enough not to grasp the absurdity of opposing suffrage because of the sex of a human being, I should be consistent enough never to raise my voice against those who have disenfranchised my brothers and myself because of race ... To assign reasons in this day and time to prove that it is unjust to withhold from one-half of the human race rights and privileges freely accorded the other half, which is neither more deserving nor more capable of exercising them, is a reflection on their intelligence.

Mary Terrell was ahead of her time in matters of shared leadership among women and men. A fan of Frederick Douglass, she took great pride in learning that he was an early and outspoken advocate of equal political rights for women. She said this of him:

> When the resolution demanding equal rights for women was introduced in the meeting held in Seneca Falls, New York, in 1848, Frederick Douglass was the only man in the convention courageous and broad-minded enough to second the motion.

Lessons Learned

The Terrell philosophy of not being afraid "to try what had not been tried" permeated team Tennessee a century ago in closing in on that thirty-sixth victory, the one that would put the Nineteenth Amendment solidly into constitutional law.

However, before Tennessee closed the deal, there was a great deal of activity in the first thirty-five states.

After Congress passed the Nineteenth Amendment, there was a rush of state ratifications. Wisconsin came in early, so did New York, Illinois, Michigan, Kansas, and Ohio. By the summer of 1919, seven more states were in the yes column, but then the campaign stalled. Meanwhile, those opposed were working to cobble together thirteen states to say "no." By January of 1920, twenty-two states had ratified. Suddenly, a cluster of ten more states approved. Some felt it had to do with the one hundredth anniversary of Susan B. Anthony's birth since she had coined the words of the amendment.

Victories followed in Oklahoma, West Virginia, and Washington to bring the approval votes to thirty-five and set the stage for the dramatic finale in Tennessee. At the same time, the antisuffrage forces were trying to reverse the original ratifications in several states. The dramatic events of those closing days and hours in Tennessee are highly relevant today.

The Tennessee women knew that when an issue is important enough, you must get organized, forming over seventy-five suffrage leagues with a membership total exceeding twenty-five thousand. And because it demanded public awareness, a communications delivery system was built by the women with marches, public meetings, and door-to-door visits—the social media of their time being very much an in-person thing. These women knew that if men elected to public office were going to be the ones making the final decision on their issue, they must lobby the men vigorously and repeatedly, even the ones who were dead set against them, so that all parties understood that this matter was not going to go away.

If we really believe in change, we can't count on someone else to make it happen—a theme the Tennessee suffragists remained loyal to throughout the years, months, days, and hours leading to the moment the lady from Niota had her letter delivered to her son, the legislator, Harry Burn.

Dear Son:
    Hurrah, and vote for suffrage! Don't keep them in doubt. I notice some of the speeches against. They were bitter. I have been watching to see how you stood, but have not noticed anything yet.
    Don't forget to be a good boy and help Mrs. Catt put the "rat" in ratification.
Your Mother

What happened that day in Tennessee—the debate, the tie vote on tabling the issue, the subsequent cliff-hanger victory, the accusations of strong-arm lobbying on both sides, and the unrestrained celebration ending seventy-two years of tenacity—is a story worth examining in every classroom in America that wishes to display democracy at its finest and most furious exercise.

> "I had rather have had a share in the battle for woman suffrage than any other world event," said **Abby Crawford Milton**, the first president of the Tennessee League of Women Voters in a letter to national leader **Carrie Chapman Catt**. "The woman suffragists have had the thrill of victory in the struggle for liberty that our ancestors had at the Declaration of Independence. It is the purest American patriotism."

The message that today's women need to preserve, as we seek to finish this job of equality for women, is that the army of suffragists in Tennessee during the first twenty years of the twentieth Century was made up of a remarkable group of willing soldiers. They included the following:

> **Mettie White** was the young legislative clerk who came up with the handwritten bill that became the Nineteenth Amendment document.

Frances Holder Overall testified before the judiciary committee in an environment not entirely receptive to women entering the voting booth.

Kate Burch Warner's advocacy of ratification became all the more admirable when it was discovered that her brother, a prominent medical school dean, was an outspoken opponent.

Lizzie Crozier French organized suffrage groups, led marches to deliver the message, and in 1920, while registering to vote, listed her occupation as "suffragist."

Elizabeth Avery Meriwether, pioneer communicator of the prosuffrage message not only in Tennessee but also throughout America, was a spellbinding speaker and advocate for the vote.

Charl Ormond Williams was a school superintendent who turned her attention to chairing the ratification campaign. She later went on to national prominence in Washington to be acclaimed as a "woman competent to hold the position of President of the United States."

These women were typical of the thousands who united to bring the Tennessee triumph to America. In honoring the past, we, at Vision 2020, believe in the lessons-learned value of finding out what it took for them to win and then applying it to the rest of what remains undone.

CHAPTER 6

Refusing to Settle

For many years, women dreamed of equal rights and, at the same time, accepted life without them. When some began to question the fairness of that system, the long trip to equality had experienced its first step.

"When a just cause reaches its flood tide, as ours has done, whatever stands in the way must fall before its overwhelming power," said Carrie Chapman Catt.

The key to her comment was the word *just*.

Every endeavor Carrie Chapman Catt took on—suffrage, international peace, and relief for war refugees—had to exhibit twin characteristics. It had to be in search of a solution to a human problem, and it had to have sufficient scope to produce significant change. In other words, it needed to be big, and it needed to be just.

A high school principal in Mason City, Iowa, in 1881, Carrie Chapman Catt survived the deaths of two husbands and went on to succeed Susan B. Anthony as president of the National American Woman Suffrage Association. In Berlin in 1904, she began a twenty-year tenure as president of the International Woman Suffrage Alliance.

With imagination and tactful leadership often heralded as second to none, she earned such respect among her colleagues that for the last quarter-century of her life (she died in 1947), she was honorary president of the League of Women Voters.

In more recent times, that comment can be expressed as "You get what you settle for." What American women have consistently been up against is an institutionalized set of behavioral habits. When we honor the past, we need to recognize that the early advocates for equal rights were confronting some monumental barriers, partly of their own construction.

How did all this happen—this exclusion of women from America's early commitment to basic human rights? Probably because there were no women in the room when the Constitution was written, so there were no women to speak up when the Constitution was debated. And there were no women called upon for their vote when the Constitution was approved.

Aside from **Abigail Adams's** letter to her husband, John, suggesting that the men forming the government should "remember the ladies," there was a total exclusion of gender equality right from the start of this new adventure called the United States of America.

The Seneca Falls Convention on Women's Rights took place more than half a century after the Constitution was constructed. It took that long for the collective unrest of three hundred women, and a few good men, to find their way to the upstate village that is now chronicled as the place where women's journey toward equality started.

Before she was twenty, **Lucretia Mott** became a teacher and almost instantly became aware that women teachers were paid less than half the salary male teachers were paid. This captured her attention, and in the 1820s, when she was not yet thirty, she began lecturing on women's equality, the abolition of slavery, and, yes, on the evils of alcohol's threat to family stability.

Her positions on those issues brought the danger of mob violence to her Philadelphia home. She was turned down as a delegate to the 1840 World Anti-Slavery Convention because she was a woman. There were threats, rejections, and anger directed her way; and they toughened the skin and bolstered the resolve of Lucretia Mott sufficiently to join Elizabeth Cady Stanton in convening the 1848 Women's Rights Convention. Already into the concept of shared leadership among women and men, she asked her husband, James, to lead the opening session.

The convention launched the women's rights and suffrage campaigns throughout the nation. Lucretia and her husband opened their home to runaway slaves; and she became an articulate speaker on peace, freedom, and equality. At eighty-seven, she delivered her final talk, six months before her death in 1880.

In spite of all the positive efforts to promote equality, many women fought against the Nineteenth Amendment.

> "We are determined," said anti-amendment advocate **Charlotte Rowe**, "to prevent women from descending to the political level of men. Passage will prostitute our civilization."

At that time, even **Eleanor Roosevelt**, who later became an ambassador of women's rights, was opposed, saying she had grown to "take it for granted that men were superior creatures and knew more about politics than women did." She changed that view in the years ahead.

Much of the early opposition came from women who feared losing their position in the family and whatever privileges that brought them. Even today, some women object to equal rights. What they overlook is that true equality permits them to make a choice about their options in life.

Financial support for the prolonged drive toward the Nineteenth Amendment was coaxed from many women and sympathetic men. However, one woman's generosity stands out—the Empress of Journalism, whose name was **Miriam Leslie**. By the time she had given up her stage career and married her third husband, the enormously successful publisher

Frank Leslie, Miriam had established herself as an excellent writer and editor. At the time of his death in 1880, Frank's publishing business was falling apart. Miriam revived it, even legally changing her name to Frank because it was easier doing business with that name. With four hundred employees and multiple publishing triumphs, she accumulated wealth and even married Oscar Wilde's brother for a year.

All around her in the early years of the nineteenth Century, the suffrage campaign was underway. She said little, but when she died in 1914, she left a million dollars "to Carrie Chapman Catt for the furtherance of the crusade for woman suffrage." A million dollars in 1914 would buy a lot of placards. It still will.

Susan B. Anthony set an example in 1872 when she cast a vote in the presidential election in Rochester, New York. She was promptly arrested, convicted, and fined—a fine she refused to pay. Many other incidents of women standing their ground for what they believed were to follow, but none quite as inspiring as what happened in Washington, DC, in 1917.

Convinced that President Woodrow Wilson had reneged on his promise to support women's suffrage, pickets gathered at the gates of the White House. Days of protest stretched into weeks, and both the chants and placards became more provocative. Thirty-two-year-old **Alice Paul** was among the 218 women arrested, and 97 were sent to prison. They endured rough treatment and were handcuffed and sentenced to the District of Columbia jail. Some drew six-month terms in the nearby Occoquan Workhouse. Alice Paul led several of the inmates on an extended hunger strike, which led to forced feedings. Through it all, pickets continued to show up at the White House.

On their release, most of those arrested took up the torch with even greater vigor. A national speaking tour called The Prison Special featured women in jail clothing campaigning for the amendment. President Wilson felt the heat and saw the light. His January 9, 1918, message in favor of women's right to vote ("Without their counseling, we shall only be half-wise.")

opened the door to House and Senate approval. He reminded the legislative bodies, "The world is watching us."

Asked later if the prison time was worth it, **Alice Paul** said, "Democracy is not always a gift. Sometimes it has to be won."

Equality for women is a goal that demands a lot. We've gone to jail, marched until our feet hurt, and absorbed all manner of verbal abuse. Still, reality tells us it's easier to get there than it is to stay there. We should know that by now.

SECTION TWO

Acting in the Present

CHAPTER 7

Building On What We've Learned

This book is about to shift into more recent history as well as the future. Hopefully, we've been listening to our sisters from the past.

We've been lucky to have these women to help us learn to welcome new ideas, invite change, and encourage innovation—all of them relentless in the pursuit of what's possible.

Their stories need to become early learning experiences for young girls. A simple semester of discovery about the leadership these women displayed can be worth a lifetime of inspiration to young girls who have often been detoured from the possibilities of their lives.

Why today's women can profit from studying the work and attitude of the women who came before us can be found by examining the value of the messages they left for us. I think of four such lessons.

Message One: They Understood Power

They knew several things about power. That it was necessary to carry out the kind of societal changes they felt were right. Complaining is a renewable resource if you find comfort in playing the victim. But if you really want to vote, be paid fairly, and have a shot at the big jobs, there is nothing quite like power.

They also knew this about power—that women didn't have any. Worse yet, in the early years of our new nation, women seemed to accept the idea that they were not entitled to any. The few women who tried to acquire power were more heavily criticized than the men who already had it and often abused it.

What most women also understood about power was that men were reluctant to surrender it, even in small quantities. People in power tend to stay in power, unless displaced by external forces.

So Elizabeth Cady Stanton and Lucretia Mott and 298 other people found their way to Seneca Falls, New York, in 1848 and produced a Declaration of Sentiments, calling for equality before the law for women. The fact that nearly two centuries have passed since they gaveled that meeting to order and we are still playing catch-up suggests we still don't understand that power can be connected to "majority rules."

Democracy today is a repetitive struggle in the U.S. Senate to win 51 votes for your side or in the House of Representatives to persuade 218 to think like you think. Democracy is imperfect. At its best, it is a balance between individual freedom and collective public behavior. Activist **Marian Wright Edelman** reminds us that "democracy is not a spectator sport."

Stanton and Mott would almost certainly wonder what we've been doing all these years. Of course, they would be proud of the Nineteenth Amendment and Title IX and pleased to see so many women in law and medicine and in leadership roles in business and government. But they might count the number of women who are CEOs in business and the number of women holding public office and ask, "Don't you know there are more women than men in America?"

Achieving equality for women is about performance, not conformance. Until the full sharing of responsibility is attained, women need to get into the habit of not being able to leave well-enough alone. Let's create, invent, learn, run for office, and rearrange our lives until we get it right. Stanton, Mott, and so many others gave us the roots and invited us to provide our own wings.

Message Two: You Don't Have to Do Everything Yourself

Challenging the way things have always been done can be an extremely lonely endeavor. The resistance to a new idea can be overwhelming, and when women began surfacing the concept of equality, objection to it resembled open warfare.

Eleanor Roosevelt characterized it this way: "Those who attack always do so with greater fervor than those who defend."

What women had to do in their early quest for fair treatment was to call attention to what was out of balance. Dissent can only be effective if you make it clear what it is you're dissenting about. And it can only be heard if a lot of other people are saying the same thing. One voice with a revolutionary idea is easily dismissed. A thousand people marching in the street, making the same point, can create a conscience-rattling echo.

That is why coalitions work. Susan B. Anthony was a spellbinding spokesperson for women's rights and suffrage. She could not, however, be everywhere. Transportation in her time was limited. There was no radio, no TV, and no internet. Her message was limited to the audience in front of her and whatever newspaper coverage she was able to generate. She knew the multiplier was in a coalition of organizations where members felt as she did, with the same goals, but who sometimes had different strategies for achieving them.

In welcoming over one hundred allied organizations to Vision 2020's campaign to advance the unfinished business of women's equality, I recognized that each group had its own agenda. That's expected, but we share a common goal.

What the women leaders of a century ago demonstrated for us was a three-part blueprint: work together in harmony (even though they did not always do this well), find goals you can agree upon (the ones that have a high degree of change are preferable), and understand that there truly is strength in numbers.

Message Three: There Is No Substitute for Tenacity

We women are at our best when doing things others say can't be done. When the odds are against us, when history has provided no clear path to follow, what has served us well is a quality relied on to overcome obstacles blocking our way to the equality goal. That quality is tenacity. It is the hinge on the door to success. It is taking one more step. It's what keeps us going when the temptation to falter, to cave in, is at its peak.

On August 26, 2020, Vision 2020 will invite Americans from coast to coast and beyond to pause for a moment and participate in a Toast to Tenacity, a salute to the seventy-two years of perseverance suffragists exhibited to win for American women the right to vote. Now known as National Women's Equality Day, the date is the centennial of the Nineteenth Amendment taking effect. Vision 2020 has been hosting this toast in Philadelphia every August, and with our Toast to Tenacity tool kit, our Delegates across the U.S. have joined us, raising glasses of grape juice in honor of the tenacity of the suffragists a century ago. Grape juice? Yes, because that's what the women of 1920, in the era of prohibition, chose as the drink to toast their victory. Wine was not an option, having been banned by the amendment just before the Nineteenth ("[T]he manufacture, sale or transportation of intoxicating liquors ... in the United States ... is hereby prohibited").

That Eighteenth Amendment was later repealed. No such fate would befall the Nineteenth. Too many people had worked too long and too hard to reverse those results.

There are many examples:

An Indiana schoolteacher, **Ida Harper**, was a journalist writing a newspaper column using a man's name. She became the voice of the suffragist campaign, an ally of Susan B. Anthony in publishing the half dozen volumes of the History of Woman Suffrage. Her continuous stream of articles and pamphlets kept alive the momentum of information on voting rights.

Eager for education, **Zora Neale Hurston** turned her Howard University education into a scholarship at Barnard, opening the door to a writing career that portrayed Black life so vividly that historians praised the national significance of her work. Her books, articles, and letters on human rights were produced through a relentless work ethic.

Born in 1938, **Janet Guthrie** reached for the unexplored. She became a pilot at seventeen, a research engineer, an astronaut candidate, and then a sports car enthusiast. As a race car driver, she overcame repeated objections to competing with men. Tenacity won out in 1978 when she placed ninth in a field of thirty-three at the Indianapolis 500 despite a broken wrist.

Tenacity—it deserves a toast.

Message Four: Do Something or Do Nothing— the Choice Is Yours to Make

After famed aviator **Amelia Earhart** disappeared during her 1937 attempt at an around-the-world flight, her husband, George Putnam, opened a letter she had left for him in the event of her death. What she wrote was "Please know that I am quite aware of the hazards. I want to do it—because I want to do it."

The decisions by breakthrough women of another time were based on their preference for action over inaction, for making something happen rather than waiting for it to happen. For now, instead of later.

Honoring the Past invites suggestions on how to bring into the public light the many women who have been standing in the shadow of history's emphasis on men's achievements. We debate the best way to highlight the splendid work of so many remarkable, but relatively unknown, women. Do we need more monuments in high-visibility places? When do women in proper numbers begin to show up on our currency? Aren't we due for some more postage-stamp recognition? How about the naming of buildings, streets, and parks? When are we going to be a part of high school and college curricula?

While all these considerations are useful, still the outcome most likely to be welcomed by the women who waged all this pioneer work would be for us to finish the job—to remove equality from the dream column and move it over to the list of norms.

In 2010, when Vision 2020 drew up its Declaration of Equality, the language was crafted from the women from the past. It was spelled out in the following words: "This declaration, inspired by the efforts of those who have come before, recognizes that although equality is in sight, it is not yet fully in place." The declaration goes on to say "[A]dvance the belief that a true sharing of leadership ... among women and men will inspire an unprecedented dimension of American excellence ... Equality is a measure of our democracy ... There is an urgency to this matter because equality delayed is opportunity denied."

The echoes ring clearly—unity, sharing, urgency, and a better nation. Those were the goals and action plans of these women we honor. We admire them, learn from them, and share with them the vision that women and men can and will grow comfortable encouraging one another to live up to individual and collective potential. We thank these women of the past. They have set us up to enrich the present.

CHAPTER 8

Balance Is Better

> We are women and men by chance. We are sisters and brothers by choice. It's time to work together for a more just and humane society. Now.

Whenever I hear a speech about the remarkable emergence of America as a great place to live, to work, and to prosper, I have two reactions. One is to agree with enthusiasm. The other is to speculate with curiosity about how much greater that American experience would be if half our government and business leaders were women.

I think of the possibilities, and I wonder, If women had an equal voice in history's choices, would there have been so many wars, so much devastation, and so much heartbreak? If Congress had 50 percent female representation all these years, would our resources have been allocated differently? Would the political turmoil and ruthless tactics that dominate our political campaigns today have become so severe? Would business be more consumer-conscious? Would women's influence on gun control and violence have changed our culture? Would adolescent girls today be growing up with more confidence in themselves if they witnessed successful women leaders all around them?

If equality had been with us from the start, would women now be evaluated the same as men—allowed to win, to lose, and to try again without the stigma that if one woman fails, we all fail?

On that last wonder, I appreciate what Michael Jordan said about the relationship of failure to success. He commented, "During my career, I missed over nine thousand shots. Often, I was given the ball for the game-ending win-or-lose shot. On twenty-seven of those occasions, I missed. My failures made possible my success."

To advance a new wave of shared leadership among women and men, two circumstances need to flourish.

One is that women who aspire to such heights in business or public office or academia or any profession must be willing and able to devote the time and tenacity it takes to be chosen for such responsibilities. **Mary Barra**, CEO of General Motors, did not just walk into the top job. She interned at eighteen, worked in human resources and communications, became a plant manager, and learned about the company's entire operation.

The second circumstance that's needed to accelerate the pace of women achieving top posts is an increase in the willingness of men to make room for them. Mentoring from leaders who have been there is critical to the people prepping to replace them. The art of decision-making should not be the permanent possession of one gender. Which of many roads to travel, when to act, and when to sit tight requires a person who is prepared with information and gifted with intuition—and unafraid to use both. That person can be a woman just as well as a man.

My conclusion from any examination of the differences between men and women is that those that do exist can be complementary and strengthen the result.

Research by Catalyst and others shows clearly that companies with more diversity among their decision-makers have better bottom lines. It stands to reason that better decisions will emerge in government also when women and men work together. As **Golda Meir** said, "Whether women are better than men I cannot say—but I can say they are certainly no worse."

In 2018, **Ellen Stofan**, a former chief scientist at NASA, was appointed to head the Smithsonian's National Air and Space

Museum. She has wonderful credentials, including a lifelong dedication to science. I was delighted to read the story, but then came the familiar message. Not four lines into the article was the phrase "will make history as the first woman to." I look forward to the day when it's no longer necessary to use "first woman to" in our language.

Vision 2020 has a simple mission: equality for women. We are committed to four goals:

Shared Leadership
Achieve fifty-fifty shared leadership among women and men in business and government

Youth Education
Educate young people to value gender equality and shared leadership

Economic Parity
Advance women's economic security by closing the gender gap in pay and retirement income

Civic Engagement
Increase the number of women who participate in the political process through voting and public service

Consistent in those goals is simplicity and the importance of more women in leadership—especially in business and government, where priorities are set and resources allocated affect all our lives.

Women are very skilled at multitasking—managing our households, our jobs, and our families. What we're not so good at is advancing our own interests. It should be clear by now that a society that craves human harmony must have more women in the places of power. We need more people who will do the right thing when there is a decision to be made. That formula has shared leadership written all over it.

Marjorie Merriweather Post's story is that of a magnificently impatient pioneer in business. For a time reference, Marjorie Post died in 1973 at the age of eighty-six. Her father had been a farm implement salesman who turned his inventive juices to breakfast cereals. In Battle Creek, Michigan, he started Postum Cereal Company and marketed Grape Nuts and Post Toasties.

His daughter Marjorie inherited that company in 1914 when she was twenty-one but couldn't sit on the board of directors because of a chromosome defect—she was a woman. However, she took an active role in the company's expansion. In 1920, she married stockbroker Edward Francis Hutton (yes, *that* E. F. Hutton), and he became chairman of Postum's board. Meanwhile, Marjorie became an early advocate of frozen foods and convinced her company to buy the patents and equipment of Clarence Birdseye. The company became General Foods. Marjorie became a philanthropist, helping hospitals, the homeless, and the performing arts.

Her shared leadership began with her father bringing her to work to show her how the business was run. She was eight years old. That strikes a memory bell for me. When my father was a U.S. Congressman, he brought me to work and showed me how the government functioned—and how sometimes it didn't. The message I got from him was that if things aren't right, don't wait too long to fix them. So if women are considering a strategy of patience, remember that history is not on our side.

CHAPTER 9

Economic Inequity Can Be Fixed

The empowerment of women is slow in achieving what we like to call economic parity. It's true at every generational level. And it's important.

I believe women and men are equally bright, and given that, why aren't they equally compensated? Why don't women enter the twilight of their lives equally assured that they can live out their days without financial worry?

Lilly Ledbetter should not have had to go through what she did. At Goodyear Tire, she was a supervisor. She had responsibility, just like the men who were also supervisors. Only she was paid 20 percent less than the men.

Unable to resolve this within the company, she went to court and won her case; but the ruling was appealed, and the case went all the way to the Supreme Court, where she lost. Lilly Ledbetter, however, did not give up. She eventually got the U.S. Congress, after a vigorous process, to pass the Fair Pay Act (they even named it after Lilly), allowing employees to challenge pay discrimination. It became the law in 2009.

The lesson learned is that you can wait around for management to correct an unfair practice or you can choose to do something about it. Lilly Ledbetter made her choice. It's a matter of seeking justice rather than waiting for things to change.

Then there was **Peggy Young** of United Parcel Service. She drove a delivery truck for four years. When she got pregnant, she was told by the doctor not to exert herself—in Peggy's case, not to lift over twenty pounds. Her paycheck vanished along with her health insurance. Peggy Young refused to accept that choosing to have a family means losing your job. She decided to see how the courts felt about that. Like Lilly Ledbetter's, Peggy's case made its way to the Supreme Court. The result: UPS changed its policy toward pregnant workers, and states all around the nation passed laws with similar protection.

Economic parity for women is about a lot more than equality in the paycheck. Most of the talk is about pay equity, the obvious fairness of paying the same salary to women and men who have the same work responsibilities. But the reality is that women often have more of the home and caregiving duties. What's missing in many circumstances are paid leave for family care; flexible work scheduling to help balance obligations to both home and employer; access to the "good jobs," those that enable a woman to enhance her income; and recognition in our Social Security system of the value of being the CEO of an American home.

What women in the workplace find, seeking somehow to lift their economic status, is that they're in a place where over 60 percent of the minimum-wage jobs are filled by women. It creates a home where a single parent with two children will need three full-time minimum-wage jobs just to stay afloat with her (or his) family expenses. It's a home where over 70 percent of mothers with children under age eighteen are in the labor force.

The gender gap in pay doesn't need to be broadcast. It needs to be corrected. And while we're equalizing things, let's not neglect a seldom-cited casualty of unequal compensation—the caregiver penalty and/or affordable care. When a woman has to take time off to care for a sick child or an aging parent, she loses ground in her career as well as loses pay.

Why do I get the feeling that with more women in high places in business and government, the likelihood of a shift in the allocation of financial resources would increase? I had to give up my job when I was pregnant with my first child in the late 1960s. It was company policy. I didn't fight it. That's just the way it was then. Thankfully, the law has stepped in on that issue.

None of us should be surprised by actions and behavior that had prevailed for two hundred years or more. Two issues were at play. One was that we had been conditioned to be treated that way. The other was that we believed what we were being taught. It became a self-inflicted downsizing of our value.

Some didn't accept what they were told and redefined the old phrase "women's work" in an entirely different way. **Megan Brennan** thought being U.S. Postmaster General was woman's work. **Michelle Howard** thought being a four-star admiral in the U.S. Navy was woman's work. **Nikki Haley** became a governor, then ambassador to the United Nations—more woman's work. **Drew Gilpin Faust** became president of an Ivy League university nearly four hundred years after Harvard discovered that, too, was woman's work.

One of humanity's most valuable pursuits—that of a homemaker and caregiver—has an underappreciated and defined job description. If Abraham Lincoln's observation is true that "Labor is the true standard of value," then running a household is way undervalued. It's time to take a look at how Social Security is structured, time to recognize real value.

Women will know when they've won equality in matters of money. We'll know when the lower-wage jobs are filled with a balance of men and women, when the penalty for caregiving is removed and access to better-paying jobs is not hindered, when Social Security credit is assigned to women who manage households, when working from home is as respected as it is accepted, and when provision is made for women who are alone in their later years and in need of dignity as well as financial security.

Recognition of the value of women needs to be much more than the month of March each year or flowers on the second Sunday in May. When regard for what we bring to the workforce is fairly rewarded by the laws and language of our land, then we can put this topic to rest. Until that day, vigilance is still on the table.

Our confidence in a positive resolution should be just as robust as our curiosity and commitment to change what needs to be changed. The outcome? Let's not kid ourselves. The rest of this road to gender equality regarding money is going to be traveled by persistence. Getting close is not enough. Throwing in the towel because of obstacles is not an option.

The message remains strong.

So much of leadership is about persistence. Staying with it. Refusing to be a dropout. Any woman who has ever worked to organize others for the purpose of equal rights will confess that more than once she has had end-of-the-day feelings like, "Am I really going to get up tomorrow morning and do this all over again?"

CHAPTER 10

Risk-Taking Is Required

> Women's voices are being heard these days in places they should have been all along—in City Halls, in Statehouses, and in Congress.

The novelty of women in public office is over. What's missing are the numbers. That's how we'll turn the volume up.

I'm not sure when I first read activist **Betty Bumpers's** words. I'm pretty certain I've never read anything else from her. I didn't have to. As far as I'm concerned, she described clearly and simply the role of women as it ought to be and did it so well that this chapter on civic engagement can only benefit from citing what she said:

> This is a time in history when women's voices must be heard or forever be silenced. It's not because we think better than men, but we think differently. It's not women against men, but women <u>and</u> men. It's not that the world would have been better if women had run it, but that the world will be better when we as women, who bring our own perspective, share in running it.

When I visit a college campus these days, I invariably find women students to be far more politically active than when I was in school. Not all of them and probably not enough of them. Still, however, there is a level of activity and awareness unheard of in my years in college. At that time, the concept of women having a significant influence in America's political agenda was remote, to say the least.

For the better part of two centuries, women in the U.S. have been mostly spectators when it comes to the government—local, state, and national. You can find exceptions in the archives, but sadly, that's just what they are—exceptions. Historically, American women have had very little influence and impact on politics and public policy.

What was true during much of the twentieth Century was that women were accustomed to the idea that power positions in the government were the exclusive purview of men. They seldom saw a woman in a high-profile government post. When I hung around Capitol Hill as a teenager, during the time my father was in Congress, my impression of our Congressional representatives was that they were all white men in dark suits.

One encouraging sign was at the U.S. State Department, where, after seventy-three men had served as Secretary of State, **Madeleine Albright** was named to the office and was followed by **Condoleezza Rice**, who was followed by **Hillary Clinton** as Secretary of State.

In 2006, **Nancy Pelosi** became Speaker of the House of Representatives. "For our daughters and granddaughters," she said, "anything is possible."

That anything-is-possible dream provides us with a view of what fifty-fifty leadership might be like. It would mean that half the leaders in our communities, half our state legislators, and half the U.S. Senate and U.S. House were women. It would mean that a woman as President and a woman as Vice President would not be uncommon.

To get there requires big numbers. Public office has to be earned by people determined enough to do the work required to win. For those thinking of running for office, these questions should help you get started.

Do You Really Think You Can Win?

Can you win? Of course, you can. Whether you're running for the School Board or a seat in Congress, never go into any venture in life thinking you're going to lose. That's an unacceptable squandering of your time and energy. When I've run for office, started community projects, and launched fundraising drives—all for the right reasons—I never went into any of these feeling I couldn't win.

Basketball coach **Pat Summitt** was asked, "How many games do you expect to win this season?" Her reply was "All of them. You asked me how many I expect to win. I've never gone into a game expecting to lose. What a message that would be to the team!"

A major motivation for women running for public office should simply be the experience of having done it. I know that in my run for the U.S. Senate in 1992, winning was a goal, but what really convinced me to enter the most turbulent adventure of my life was my post–Anita Hill commitment: an I-must-do-this incentive.

Donna Shalala, whose credentials include being university president at Wisconsin and Miami, plus Secretary of U.S. Health and Human Services, decided in her late seventies to run for Congress in 2018 (she won). I asked her what her motivation was, given that she had already achieved so much. Her response was "I was pissed off!"

Whatever drives you—existing conditions you want to change or a determination to add to women's chances of getting to fifty-fifty—those reasons are good enough. No matter what happens with the ballot count, you're a winner for trying.

What Is It about Public Service that Appeals to You?

It probably isn't the money. It's not likely the hours will hold much attraction. If you enjoy the prospect of constituents shouting at you or sending angry emails, elective office may be your thing. The question you may want to ask yourself is this: "Are you in public service, or is public service in you?"

Public service can change things that need changing. It's an arena where you can do a lot to protect the young, to help the elderly live in dignity, to bring about equality in and out of the workplace, and to promote better health, clean air, and clean water—a more just and peaceful society.

If you have an interest in politics and public service, trust that intuition. Your intuition is the sum total of the values you care about. It is the product of all that is important to you. Let it guide you.

Does Family Help or Hinder a Career in Politics?

On the question of family, the short answer is that you do not have to sacrifice your family life for your public life. It requires some juggling of your time, but women have a natural, built-in instinct for balancing multiple agendas. It comes with the territory. What matters is that if both your family life and your civic engagement activity are important to you, as they are to me, you'll find a way to make them compatible companions.

However, I caution that fitting your family life into your public life is not some mathematical formula that magically offers precise allocations of your time to each interest. It's more a matter of some blending of the two and a lot of communicating. Remember, First Amendment rights apply also to your family. Your family members have a right to their privacy, so it's useful to keep in mind that the key to having a personal life is not answering unnecessary questions about it.

What Are Your Reasons for Wanting to Do This?

Getting involved or running for office or simply engaging in how you're governed is one decision that requires early self-examination. When it became my time to deal with this question, I thought about two issues, which were also questions: Why, with a governmental system that permits individual freedom and opportunity envied by the world, do we struggle so hard to persuade people to enter politics and public service? And why, with a growing nation that has triple the population it had when I was born and where the stakes are so high for all of us, do we struggle to keep the political pipeline filled with good people who aspire to leadership?

In considering those two questions, I discovered that maybe I was among those settling for less than I could contribute. I had some ideas. I had some visions about a better tomorrow. I was not afraid of the political process, having grown up with it. Maybe I ought to run for office or visibly support candidates I agree with. That is the test you put yourself through.

Remember, I've said there are no losers when women compete in the office-seeking portion of our democracy. That's a hard point to sell to a woman who has spent the better part of a year smiling so much her jaws hurt.

In the Spring of 2018, a refreshing number of women ran for various offices in the Pennsylvania primaries. When the election was over, I wrote congratulatory notes to those who had come in first and also to those who ran but came up short in the vote count. From the primary winners who would be continuing on in their campaigns for the November balloting, I received polite and gracious responses. But the really emotional messages of appreciation came from those who did not win. I had thanked them for running, for setting an example, and for attempting something they previously felt they could not do.

What Special Qualities Do You Have that Will Appeal to Voters?

This is a question you don't leave to yourself. If you compile the list, you are almost certain to shortchange yourself. This job of putting together an inventory of your assets belongs to your friends. Let those who know you best confirm your integrity, tenacity, compassion, leadership, valor, and all those other traits you've been developing for so long. Getting involved in your community or your country was never intended to be a solo flight. You'll need others around you who can see what you might be too modest to mention.

The other end of that thought is to have people who will share with you the speed bumps in your character, those who will talk to you about what needs to be tuned—your voice, your knowledge of the issues, or your approach to fundraising. Politics will teach you how to be friends with more than one person at a time.

What Will You Do Differently in the Job?

Asking yourself what you will do differently is the first draft of your plan for change or platform. Whatever you call it, what should emerge is a clear set of proposals, actions that reflect what you want to see changed. It's what spurred you to get into this competition. And make it clear that you will work harder than anyone has before to achieve the agenda.

Do You Understand How Much Money You Will Need?

When I contacted the well-known political consultant James Carville in late 1991 about running for the U.S. Senate, his first question was "Do you have money?" Three things are worth remembering: (a) financial backing is right up there with oxygen—and you'll need a team who can raise money, count it, and keep you from turning your home over to the bank; (b) avoid comparing your resources with those of your opponent—it takes time explaining why you have less or why you aren't doing as well in the polls even though you've raised more money; and (c) do the math—one donor giving one thousand dollars is nice, but one hundred giving ten dollars is the same amount and nets you one hundred voters (the best solution is to receive both).

It's not easy for women in politics to raise money. For one thing, we're not used to talking about money, much less asking for it. The network of connections that men have built over a lifetime are not as readily available to most women. Sometimes we don't help one another as much as we should. That's a shame because women are good at coalitions, and organizations like EMILY's List have made a huge difference. When we get it together, we are unstoppable. Supporting women candidates through donations, volunteering time, or just putting up a yard sign is invaluable and is another way to contribute to change.

Can You Handle the Heat?

This is a question to think hard about. Have no illusions. Be prepared. You will see yourself quoted saying things you never said. You will be called names you haven't heard since high school when you didn't know what they meant. If you ever tried to smuggle a dozen items into the grocery ten-itemsor-less line, somebody will have found out about it in what they call opposition research.

The political road for women is constantly under construction. It is dotted with potholes. It is a toll road. If you're not tough enough, you're going to be looking for the nearest exit ramp. There are people out there eager to catch you in the slightest mistake. All that isn't right. But it's real.

So why do it? Because it's worth it. Women throughout history have been brave when they had to be. If we are to enrich the present, today's women will do the same thing. Besides, when you commit to civic engagement, your sight improves. You can see things not previously apparent. You can see a day when legislatures have gender balance, when a woman on the presidential ballot—maybe two of them—is no shock to America.

No matter what the outcome of a woman's entry into politics, if you care enough about the change you're trying to create, you will take what you learned and continue the fight. The hours are long. The challenge is continual. The expectations are high. But the goal is priceless.

Thank you, **Shirley Chisholm, Geraldine Ferraro,** and **Hillary Clinton.** You were willing to take the heat in the most glaring of spotlights and move us all closer to where women have never been.

CHAPTER 11

What If All Women Voted?

What better way to enrich the present and celebrate the centennial of the Nineteenth Amendment than to set a goal of 100 percent turnout of eligible women voters in the 2020 election? Preposterous idea. Can't be done. Or how close can we come?

From its beginning, America has been a grand social experiment. The only Native Americans are the American Indians. Everyone else got here by boat or plane or because their ancestors did. Yet nearly all share a single purpose—to be free to pursue their chosen lives. Freedom, of course, is not free. Good sense teaches us that. Good citizenship demands that we know it.

Voting in local, state, and national elections is how the individual influences how she or he is governed. Voting is a noble endeavor. It gives us a stake in the way the country runs. When it's really at its best, with citizens together, almost any problem we face can be solved.

We have come too far as a nation to devalue our freedom by neglecting to vote. Too much blood has been spilled in wars fought to protect that freedom for us to squander the elective process. Yet that very freedom permits us not to vote, if that is our choice.

Sadly, millions exercise that choice not to vote. Ask them why and they'll say,

"I don't know who is running"
or

"I don't like any of the candidates"
or
"My vote doesn't matter"
or
"I couldn't get to the polls."

These are all lame excuses, but they're frequently heard.

President John F. Kennedy was one of the first politicians to inspire me with his words. About the time I was graduating from college, he gave a speech to the United Nations. He said, "Never before have we had such capacity to control our own environment, to end thirst and hunger, to conquer poverty and disease, to banish illiteracy and massive human misery."

It was one of the last speeches President Kennedy gave. Shortly thereafter, he was assassinated in Dallas, a victim of the very violence his leadership was pledged to try to end. I remember one of the prime reasons he went to Dallas. It wasn't to stage a pep rally for the people of Texas. He went there to patch up some hard feelings among people who held differing views in his own political party.

I credit him, along with my father, of course, with some of my early interest in public service. I think of his "never before have we had such capacity" when I ponder the positive change that women can bring to the nation. Every minute we devote to squabbling among ourselves, every hour we hold a grudge over turf, every Election Day we ignore our opportunity to express our citizenship—all that adds up to time lost.

We women should treasure the vote. Our half of the population waited seemingly forever to win it. Yet we seldom exceed 65 percent of our potential. Still, since 1964, women have regularly cast more ballots than men.

The observations above are focused on general election performance. What's far worse is the turnout—male and female—for primary elections, where the people who will run in November are selected. I think of the primary in New York City in June of 2018, a celebrated congressional election, because a twenty-eight-year-old woman candidate—**Alexandria Ocasio-Cortez**—upset a twenty-plus-year incumbent.

Television newscasters and commentators broke out their most extravagant phrases. Social media lit up. Newspapers went to the big print headlines. Party leaders debated the significance. Lost in all this turbulence was the fact that the election attracted a 22 percent turnout of voters. Carry the math a little further. The winner polled over half of that 22 percent figure, which means that the Congressional representative from that district of New York got her start by winning just over one of every ten eligible voters. Sobering. There was nothing wrong with her win. She worked hard and won enough votes to post the upset. Her supporters justifiably celebrated.

What couldn't be celebrated was the dismal turnout.

"I don't measure America by its achievement, but by its potential," said **Shirley Chisholm.**

"What people want is very simple—they want an America as good as its promise," said **Barbara Jordan.**

"America, which has the most glorious present still existing in the world today, hardly stops to enjoy it, in her insatiable appetite for the future," said **Anne Morrow Lindbergh.**

All three of these comments, plus some around-the-table conversation with colleagues, inspired a surge of unconventional goal-setting at Vision 2020 early in 2016. Vision 2020 was founded to help finish the women's equality agenda of the suffragists. Our work put its emphasis on shared leadership among women and men, economic security for women at all stages of their life, education to teach young people about women's history and to value gender equality, and women's increased civic engagement with particular emphasis on voting and public service.

During our planning sessions with Vision 2020 Delegates from coast to coast, it became clear that there were a number of organizations keenly involved in registering people to vote.

What we saw was an opportunity to connect those organizations and the need for a comprehensive communications program to persuade women that the pathway to power ran through the ballot box.

Thus emerged the Vision 2020 goal. In honor of the one hundredth anniversary of the Nineteenth Amendment, Vision 2020's Women 100 National Celebration seeks a 100 percent turnout of eligible women voters for the November 2020 general election.

Democrats. Republicans. Independents. Every registered woman voter.

Some people say, "You'll never reach 100 percent. That's impossible." But most people applaud the goal. What bolsters my optimism is the lesson learned from many years of running fundraising campaigns. In setting a goal, think big! It's more productive to raise 80 percent of a million-dollar goal than 100 percent of a half-million-dollar target.

I am a believer in historian Arnold Toynbee's theory that the value of the goal lies in the goal itself, that the goal cannot be attained unless it is pursued for its own sake. The possibilities of a competitive campaign among the states or among other competing institutions to see which can emerge as the top turnout producer in the 2020 election seems to me to be a good strategy. Stay tuned for the results after November 3, 2020!

We're in the company of all who find worth in being loyal to the belief that we must keep fresh in America's memory one of our nation's most historic acts of self-sacrifice—seventy-two years of gallantry by the suffragists. And we need to remember the prominent women throughout history who toiled in relative obscurity but stayed with the struggle because the goal of equality for women was so important. There are 150-million-plus women and girls in the U.S. today capable of being inspired to put the year 2020 forever in the history books as the time America established once and for all time that power works best when it's shared.

So how does one picture 100 percent of eligible women voting?

First, to be clear, one is not eligible to vote unless she or he is registered to vote. So the goal is to register as many women as possible, working closely with the many organization doing nonpartisan voter registration, and then to make sure those eligible registered women actually vote.

This should not be so difficult. Two factors seem to motivate such behavior. One is that voting provides a good feeling, a sense of doing something responsible. Add the emphasis that in 2020, you're expressing your appreciation to women of a century ago who won this right for us. Never let it be doubted that it was *won*—nobody *gave* it to us.

A second motivating factor is the awareness that we are part of something large and historic. There is momentum present in a quest to do something that's never been tried. There is also the competitive climate that Vision 2020 will create.

Like any major undertaking, the key is to break the mountain down into foothills, to make the Women 100% project manageable.

Fortunately, Vision 2020 has footprints in each state, plus over 100 Allied Organizations that share some or all the equality agenda. Prominent among those allies, for example, is the League of Women Voters, which got its start at about the same time the Nineteenth Amendment's ink was drying.

What is also essential is a massive information program to inform every woman of what we're trying to do—traditional radio, television, newspapers, and of course, social media. We have designed a special tool for smartphones and laptops. Wherever people get their information becomes fair game: Children bringing home a note from school reminding adults to vote, faith leaders adding a message to their sermons, a visual display in every supermarket, billboards, or town meetings.

How close can American women get to the 100-percent goal?

As planned, all those results are to be announced mid-November in 2020, two weeks after the general election. Part of what fascinates me as a one-time political candidate myself is the nonpartisan nature of the 100-percent campaign. It's not about Republicans, Democrats, or Independents. It is about women and our willingness to honor the past, enrich the present, and shape the future.

In 2018, at our request, Pennsylvania Governor Tom Wolf took the lead by inviting the forty-nine other governors to join in the Vision 2020 campaign. His letter included this:

> Since this is a national celebration, Vision 2020 invites the participation of every state ... There will be programs that every state can support locally, such as the Toast to Tenacity on Women's Equality Day (August 26) and a voter registration, education and mobilization campaign to turn out eligible women to vote in record numbers for the 2020 national election—a "thankyou" to the suffragists of a century ago and demonstration of women's collective commitment to increased civic engagement.

The Toast to Tenacity reference is also a national spotlight event in 2020. For a number of years, Vision 2020 has staged a toast to the suffragists every August. Carried out properly in 2020, the nation will pause for a moment and raise glasses in tribute to the valiant women of another time.

No champagne. The Eighteenth Amendment forbade "the manufacture, sale or transportation of intoxicating liquor." It was called Prohibition. That amendment was overturned by the Twenty-First Amendment, which repealed the Eighteenth and was ratified with lightning speed, but I've always thought that with Prohibition, the nation must have sobered up and granted women's voting rights.

Now it's up to us to convince women to exercise that right.

CHAPTER 12

Enriching the Present

> There are three kinds of people: those who make things happen, those who watch things happen, and those who have no idea what happened. Women need to be in the first category.

In 2013, on the occasion of the twentieth anniversary of the Institute for Women's Health and Leadership at Drexel University in Philadelphia (the home of Vision 2020), **Dr. Bernice Sandler**, the Godmother of Title IX, was awarded an honorary degree by Drexel President John Fry. He said of her,

> She was fearless enough to file the first charges of sex discrimination against 250 institutions in the 1970s; persistent enough to get the attention of Congress and give the first testimony before a Congressional Committee about discrimination against women in education; dedicated enough to devote her life to educational equity for women.

When people ask me what I mean by "enriching the present," I simply mention Bernice Sandler. She clearly fulfills the enriching definition of confronting a situation as it is and then finding a way to make it better.

"Forty years ago," Dr. Sandler said, "if somebody told me I would be getting an honorary degree, I would have laughed hysterically. Before I became involved in women's issues, the two things I wanted to do included being an assistant to some great man and to be very ladylike. I gave those goals up a while back."

She continued, "Title IX is the most important law passed for women and girls since women got the right to vote in 1920. It's part of the women's movement and has worldwide impact. This is a revolution as great as the industrial revolution. We're going to see men and women able to have relationships based on respect and friendship. We will not finish all this change in our lifetimes, but we have taken the first steps of what is going to be a very long, but worthwhile, journey."

Determined to defeat collegiate sexism, Dr. Sandler teamed up with Oregon Congresswoman **Edith Green** and Hawaiian Congresswoman **Patsy Mink** to bring home the Title IX legislation in 1972. What became enriched was campus life in terms of eliminating discrimination in admissions, hiring, and also in the funding of women's athletic programs.

The result is that it's illegal to deny admission to college because you are a woman. More than half of college students today are women. Majority rules!

Title IX also created increased athletic opportunities for girls and women, including scholarships and facilities, resulting in a dramatic boost in self-confidence. Think engineering and science. Think soccer and basketball. Think doctors and lawyers.

Enriching the present is not limited to major legal change. What is available to each of us every day is an opportunity to change things that need changing.

Maybe it's the need for a safer playground or a workplace situation that's obviously unfair. Create a wish list—things that needs to be improved. Then you can figure out how you can begin to bring change. By now, women should be beyond the stage of staying silent when we see an injustice. Silence implies approval. Those of us who are mothers are natural advocates for our children. We need to speak up for ourselves and other women too.

You don't have to run for office to make change. You don't have to be a CEO of a major business or a partner in a professional firm. While those might be nice, they're not necessary to carry out your own enriching mission. Remember, we're talking about taking something and making it better. That may be the open position on a local board. It may be a neighborhood improvement campaign. It may be a one-time fundraising event.

Enriching the present is about leadership now. There are many people thinking about getting involved next year as soon as they get the time. In the 1940s, a survey listed the top seven discipline problems in public schools as talking, chewing gum, making noise, running in the halls, getting out of turn in line, wearing improper clothes, and not putting paper in wastebaskets. By 1980, the top seven had changed to drug use, alcohol abuse, pregnancy, suicide, rape, robbery, and assault. Times change, but one thing doesn't—the need for leadership to make bad things good and good things better.

There is much to be done—improving our health care system, making good education available to all young people, achieving fair pay, and getting more women in leadership positions. Much of that will be accomplished through communication—sometimes by one voice, most of the time by many voices united by the same message.

This chapter started with the amazing contributions of Bernice Sandler, who sparked a turning-point breakthrough in equality for women. How important was communication to her? She published 3 books and 100 essays and gave 2,500 speeches. Ideas create changes. Words set them in motion.

Each woman, in her own way, has the daily opportunity to be an enricher by standing up for our beliefs, speaking out on the things we deem important, working with others on improving the community, and committing to have a positive answer if anyone asks, "What have you done to enrich the present?"

Shortly after becoming Director of the Institute for Women's Health and Leadership at Drexel University College of Medicine in 2002, I wanted to put an exclamation mark on the interconnectedness of the two parts of our name. In my thinking, you can't have women's health without women's leadership, and vice versa. We created the Woman One program to honor women of exceptional leadership characteristics.

To add value, we decided to add the health factor by using Woman One to raise money for medical school scholarships for underrepresented women seeking to become physicians. Woman One became an instant success. Our scholarships started out at sixty thousand dollars over four years and are now up to one hundred thousand dollars. Thirty-two young women from all over America, some with origins in Africa and Latin America, have become Woman One Scholars, and many graduates are practicing medicine in underserved areas. We keep in touch with them. Their stories define what enriching the present really means.

In 2020, in support of Vision 2020's commitment to Shared Leadership among women and men, we have created an additional scholarship named for our exceptional mentor and friend, Dr. Walter Cohen, who died in 2018. The D. Walter Cohen Shared Leadership Scholarship was designed for an underrepresented man studying medicine at Drexel, and in the spirit of Title IX, which prohibits sex discrimination, we will make both the Cohen and Woman One scholarships available to underrepresented students regardless of gender.

Over the years, I've found that women are particularly adept at looking at an idea and figuring out what more it can be. That's the essence of enriching.

SECTION THREE

Shaping The Future

CHAPTER 13

Coalitions Are Crucial

People ask me how Vision 2020 began. The truth is that I was tired of the slow pace of progress for women. Often it seemed like two steps forward, three steps back. To change that, something different had to happen.

I have never been known for my patience. I don't like standing in line or waiting for my name to be called. When that feeling of powerlessness is extended to an entire gender, it's only a matter of time and temper before the urge for a change overcomes the reluctance to seek one. In pursuing equality for women in America, we're dealing with a supply problem. We have an oversupply of doubt about a future that features shared leadership among women and men and an undersupply of people willing to work together to achieve such a balance. That's the challenge.

We need the fundamental foundation of a future where equality is a way of life instead of a distant dream. Although Americans have been historically much better at dealing with crisis than preventing it, I sense that we are about to discover how rewarding it can be when we combine our inherited spirit of independence with a lively new spirit of initiative.

What makes America unique is that each of us has nearly unlimited choices to make:

- We can choose to develop our know-how, or we can watch others develop theirs. And in a future well-shaped, we'll help one another unselfishly.

- We can choose to be active in our schools, our communities, and our country; or we can let other people make all the decisions that affect our lives (and then complain about most of them).
- We can choose to respect one another as women and men and pass on that trait to our children, or we can be suspicious of the other person's motives.

To have this future where the talents and brainpower of all people are fully engaged, some things will have to change. One of those things is our language. Thankfully, that change is already underway. One example is the Presbyterian hymnal in my church in which several years ago, the new version was introduced with references to "mankind," male pronouns, and other sexist language replaced with gender-neutral words and phrases.

Some expressions familiar to women are in the process of being retired. Part of women distancing ourselves from the language of the past has to do with more women in leadership, the enlightenment of employers, the change in laws, and the awakening that we simply aren't going to accept it anymore. We can dream about a perfect society, even preach about it, and sometimes joke about our human futility in trying to achieve it; but what women are really seeking is a climate that fulfills the essential elements of equality. We may visualize perfection, but we'll settle for fairness.

In return for this fairness, this opportunity to compete and contribute free of historic restraints, women can commit to bringing four qualities to this pursuit of a more harmonious civilization: loyalty, integrity, service, and generosity. Any woman who wants to have a hand or heart in the shaping of the future should possess these qualities.

- Loyalty to a cause or a conscience
- Integrity in our words and deeds

- Service to an agenda larger than ourselves and encouraging others to do the same
- Generosity in giving what we have—time, talent, support, and, yes, money to advance our values

I was thinking about the slow pace of women's progress when I went to sleep one night in 2008. When I woke up at 3:00 a.m., which I maintain is the hour of the day that produces the best ideas, my mind had edited itself down to a thought so obvious, so promising in its development, that it kept me awake the rest of the night.

It may have been because I was scheduled to attend a meeting at Philadelphia's National Constitution Center (NCC) the next day or perhaps because the Obama campaign for president was stimulating a national conversation on race, but it became clear to me that America had never had a national conversation about gender equality. I realized that we were only twelve years away from the hundred-year anniversary of women's voting rights, and I knew I needed to talk to people about that in our meeting at the Constitution Center. That was the logical starting point because the Center focus is the document that provided the governing guide for the nation. It was also the document that, in its 1787 configuration, ignored women and people of color—more than half the U.S. population.

We were meeting with the Center's staff about showcasing a traveling exhibit on women in medicine. As Director of the Institute for Women's Health and Leadership at Drexel University's College of Medicine, I was accompanied by the College Historian. I couldn't help bringing up the conversation-on-women's-equality idea. The NCC's National Program Director at that time, Jane Eisner, was interested, and we began to discuss a national campaign for women's equality—what was to become Vision 2020.

By 2010, Vision 2020 had Delegates in all fifty states and a number of Allied Organizations. We convened this national coalition at the NCC and launched "An American Conversation about Women and Leadership." A Vision 2020 agenda was developed, with four parts:

- Shared Leadership among Women and Men—Increasing the number of women in senior leadership positions in business and government
- Economic Parity—Closing the gender gap in pay and retirement income
- Youth Education—Educating young people to value gender equality, shared leadership, and civic engagement
- Civic Engagement—Increasing women's participation in the political process through voting and public service

The first Vision 2020 Congress—there have been five more—claimed a front-row seat in my memory theater. Extraordinary women leaders from all states gathered to advance women's equality. The Congress immediately took to its connecting duty—connecting individuals, organizations, issues, and resources.

That 2010 Congress introduced Vision 2020's Declaration of Equality:

> This declaration, proclaimed by American women united in purpose, commends to this nation the wisdom and obligation of achieving equality.
>
> This declaration, inspired by the efforts of those who have come before, recognizes that although equality is in sight, it is not yet in place. We are dedicated to enabling children to reach adulthood with full expectations of equality, advances the belief that a true sharing of leadership and responsibility among women and men will inspire an unprecedented dimension of American excellence.

> This declaration contends that without equality we cannot truly claim that we the people are fairly self-governed and free to pursue happiness. Equality is both a measure of our democracy and its hallmark. It is the foremost feature of justice and it is descriptive of our common humanity. There is an urgency to this matter because equality delayed is opportunity denied.
>
> This declaration, signed by willing hands pledged to devote their time, talent and tenacity to the fulfillment of all that equality promises, is now submitted to the hearts, minds and collective conscience of the American people.

I revisit the words occasionally to refresh myself on the high worth of our mission.

Subsequent congresses were held by Vision 2020 in Chicago, Portland, Philadelphia, Nashville, and Miami. In Chicago, we made a special effort to honor organizations that had excelled in shared leadership, providing examples of how the decision-making skills of women and men can be utilized to maximum benefit. In Portland, we celebrated pioneer breakthroughs by women in a state where both the vote and women in high places were well ahead of the curve. In Nashville, we remembered the state that delivered the clinching vote for the Nineteenth Amendment. And in Miami, a city of textbook diversity, we were reminded that in any plans to shape a better future, all girls and all women must be included in the equalizing of opportunity.

The grand Congress of them all is in Philadelphia in September of 2020, the high-water mark of a full Vision 2020 year of celebrating the centennial of the Nineteenth Amendment. That celebration, Women 100, will provide a national report card on progress toward equality. Vision 2020 has put down a lot of footprints since its beginning. Now we have Delegates across the nation and are allied with over one hundred other nonprofit, nonpartisan organizations united behind a goal toward which we're all sailing.

CHAPTER 14

What Equality Looks Like

The tyranny of precedent is keenly responsible for the phrase "We've always done it this way." Pretty soon, entire generations can grow up thinking there is no other way.

If equality for women is to become a reality, we must pay the price of achieving it; and the longer we postpone it, the more certain we are to discover that the price keeps getting higher. It's no bargain right now, but delay will only make us wish we had acted sooner.

Change is not something to fear. It is something to manage with a belief that whatever the hurdle, we can overcome it. The foundation of democracy provides us with a system where we can debate and disagree with one another but still operate with a consensus. That's a formula for deciding what the change we want really looks like. Then we can determine what sacrifices we are willing to make, what dreams we are committed to pursue, and what human values are important to us.

So what does equality look like?

I've been able to imagine it through some mental photographs—pictures that have not been taken.

A vivid mental photo from my youth is a U.S. Congress made up of men. At age five, I sat with my father on the floor of the House of Representatives to listen to President Truman deliver a State of the Union address. During the twenty-two years that my father served in the House, I spent many hours on Capitol Hill listening to committee hearings and working in Congressional offices during my high school summers. I do not recall seeing any women or people of color in that decision-making body.

I'm a fan of the annual State of the Union message, delivered by the President to a joint session of Congress. It doesn't matter who's in power. I'll be in front of my TV set, where I can see the Senate, the House, members of the Supreme Court, and the President's cabinet all in one room. An impressive picture. But the picture I want to see is one where out of every two people sitting there, one is a woman. And a woman at the podium would be nice. That photo awaits the change that defines equality.

The second photograph I want to put into my album would be a composite picture of the Fortune 500 chief executive officers. The 500 issue is a much-anticipated Fortune publication. It is a way business keeps score. What's missing is the photo of the 500 CEOs, and what's really missing from my imagined photo of the current list is a shocking imbalance of gender.

What does equality look like? In most cases, it looks like a fifty-fifty sharing of decision-making responsibilities and results. It's not competition between women and men, but between individual human beings. Sometimes the man will win, sometimes the woman. Sometimes **Billie Jean King** will beat Bobby Riggs.

In our American democracy, equality for women shouldn't take so long to achieve, especially when we have so many examples of women who have already refused to accept a secondary status in their lives. One of the ways I determine what equality looks like is to look around me at women who have found it—women who live their lives not in the shadow cast by men but as independent, self-reliant individuals.

My work with Vision 2020 has enabled me to encounter many such women all across the United States. Their leadership examples are inspiring. I could name hundreds, but I will highlight four. I met each of these women at the first Vision 2020 Congress in 2010, and they continue to play key leadership roles today.

Deborah Brittain

This unique leader has never backed down from a challenge and never overlooked an opportunity to communicate to others what the combination of talent, vision, and hard work can accomplish. In the early years of Vision 2020, she clearly understood the mission from the start. "The very idea of assembling strong, confident women for the purpose of advancing equality," she said, "appeals to me in so many ways." Always there as a major donor, as a willing adviser, and as a go-anywhere communicator, Deborah's commitment to Vision 2020 is clearly a continuation of a life of leadership.

Ask Howard University where she earned her Bachelor's degree and Simmons School of Social Work where her Master's followed. Ask the people of Preod Corporation, a firm that finds and places business executives, where she was Executive Vice President. Her leadership graced the Association of Junior Leagues International, serving as president during their centennial. She was on the advisory board of Harvard Business School. She brought her energy to organizations dealing with kidney disease and with the blind. Add in her alliance with the Salvation Army and the National Council of Negro Women and the Northern Virginia Urban League.

That partial listing for a woman of exceptional enthusiasm and the know-how to back up her confidence explains my instant admiration. Hear her speak, and you will understand that she's already arrived at the equality destination. Watch her work, and you will sense her willingness to help others make the trip.

Susan Butler

This is a woman who has lived her life as if she's double-parked in every positive aspect of that multivalued assessment—management consultant, technology expert, philanthropist, author, speaker, and consistently among the first to raise her hand on Vision 2020 initiatives to put women's equality on the fast track.

Susan Butler never took time to find out there was an equality obstacle. She was too busy becoming Arthur Andersen's first professional female employee, only a preview to being named the first woman Partner of what is now known as Accenture. Susan served on Accenture's principal advisory and strategy-setting committee and as President of the Accenture Foundation.

As a philanthropist, she has endowed academic chairs and scholarships. Her work at Purdue University, the home of so many of America's astronauts, is part of the reason the Governor of Indiana singled her out for the distinguished Wabash award, a citation often reserved for U.S. presidents, ambassadors, and astronauts. As versatile as she is professionally, Susan's support web embraces a wide range of national action programs, including the Girl Scouts of the USA, Junior Achievement, and happily, Vision 2020.

She authored two books with a top ten title, which I cherish: *Women Count: A Guide to Changing the World* and *Become the CEO of You, Inc.* The titles invite you. The lessons inside challenge you to do what she did—to approach each day with an unbending philosophy of "I see no glass ceiling." Though she now suffers from dementia, her life suggests that we don't wait around for the miracle to happen. Whatever distant music drove her convinced her that equality awaits those who claim it.

Barbara Roberts

It would be difficult to find a woman who could match Barbara Roberts's story in terms of Vision 2020 goals of shared leadership and civic engagement.

On civic engagement, she became Governor of Oregon, elected to that office in 1990, the first woman voted in to lead that state. But as they say in Oregon, that election was not her first rodeo. Previously, she served in the Oregon House of Representatives for four years, two of them as Majority Leader, and then won election as Secretary of State. Barbara was no stranger to hotly contested campaigns from school board to state capital. She demonstrated that a woman leader under the high pressure of tough policy decisions could be poised, strong, and forceful. Her public personality added a bonus. She has a warmth and sense of humor that I treasure. Her willingness to answer the Vision 2020 call and bring her wisdom to our campaign for women's equality was an early boost.

On shared leadership, she understood the value of equal footing with men. "In order for women to win their right to vote," she said, "men had to play a major part. All legislators were male in those days, and getting over half of them to vote in favor was necessary for passage in many states." She urges all women to understand the worth of the ballot. ("I feel strongly that our vote is our voice. If I don't vote, my views remain silent. When I cast my vote, I express my positions as a citizen, as an Oregonian, as an American.")

If I had to limit myself to one title to describe Barbara Roberts, it would be Communicator. She is a nationally recognized public speaker and author. Her topics are not restricted to her breakthrough experiences in public office, although her book *Up the Capitol Steps* is considered a significant contribution to Oregon history. She also wrote an award-winning book—*Death without Denial, Grief without Apology*—about end-of-life challenges. Like nearly every step in her life, this was done with her own special warmth and compassion.

Kim Olson

Her story is as big and dynamic as the Texas she adores. I knew she was the kind of changemaker Vision 2020 needed the first time I read what this Air Force Colonel said about women of the early 1980s: "Women in that era, whether it was in the military or in other of life, didn't just open doors—we took them off the hinges." Bold enough to give up a prospective teaching career to join the Air Force. Bold enough to insist on becoming a pilot when she was discouraged at almost every turn. Bold enough to one day command her own squadron where her leadership skills were tested every day, every mission.

"The Air Force, like most institutions, doesn't just survive. It thrives when it has diversity," she said. "Diversity simply makes for a better society."

When she retired after a brilliant career that included a high-level duty in the Pentagon, she moved to Texas and took a job as Director of Human Resources for the Dallas Independent School District, the second largest district in Texas. I met her when she was president of Grace After Fire, an organization dedicated to helping women veterans. When I asked her to join a Vision 2020 trip to Scotland for an international conference on women in war, she was on the next plane.

In 2014, Kimberly Olson was inducted into the Texas Hall of Fame; and four years later, with public service on her mind, she ran for election as Texas Secretary of Agriculture. Although she did not win that race, she's now a candidate for the U.S. Congress in 2020.

Her advice to girls and women: "When you're the first at something, you need to get used to the idea that you're always being watched, and some people will look for you to fail. You have to hang tight. If you quit, you'll prove them right, and there won't be hope for you or the women after you."

Brittain, Butler, Roberts, and Olson—four distinctly individual achievers, each with her own style. Put them together, and you have a quartet of trailblazers capable of inspiring thousands. What Vision 2020 seeks to do is bring together many more of these women and benefit from their collective brainpower.

That assembly should present America with a resounding picture of what equality for women really looks like. The picture is clear enough for leaders to guide those who are still uncertain of the path. We should see it as much as an obligation as it is an opportunity. We should remind the nation's young that getting there is not somebody else's job but rather requires the energy of all.

CHAPTER 15

Overcoming Obstacles

A woman standing on the bank of a river sees another woman on the opposite bank. The first woman shouts, "How do I get to the other side of the river?" The second woman shouts back, "You are on the other side of the river!" When you're shaping a plan, perspective is important.

Rosemarie Greco is a woman with perspective and wisdom. In almost every new challenge I've taken on, she has been there with her loyalty, her thoughtfulness, and her unparalleled insight—at times, when most needed.

She is a woman of exceptional competence. Her confidence and judgment earn and demand respect in and out of the workplace. She knows how to run a meeting and how to run a company. She believes that the power to fulfill the next responsibility is a reward for accomplishing the last one.

Rosemarie is no stranger to the campaign for women's equality. Formerly the highest-ranking woman in banking in the U.S., she knows the feeling of being the only woman in the boardroom. She has made the lonely CEO decisions that influence the lives of customers, shareholders, employees, and their families. She understands the fine line between healthy debate and arrogant outbursts.

"Dreams are about beautiful things," she said. "Life is about duty."

More than once, I experienced close-up what she meant. I saw her courage in standing with me when the early challenges of the Women's Way umbrella funding experiment were underway. I saw her loyalty in supporting my 1992 run for the U.S. Senate. I saw her generosity in terms of time, talent, and money when we began the Vision 2020 endeavor to close the deal once and for all on equality for women.

Now, as she and I both confront the reality of a relentless calendar where the torn-off pages don't get replaced—a time we like to call the Springtime of our maturity—it's clear we both share similar pride in the advances women have made so far and similar unrest about all that remains undone. We recognize that the last defense against aging is a life that continues to chase goals that have meaning. Trying to improve economic, social, and civic opportunities for women embraces such goals. A vacuum can only exist in our lives if we permit it.

Rosemarie Greco's blend of reality-based judgment and social conscience is exactly what's needed to clear the hurdles to women's equality. And there is no getting around the reality that obstacles to women's equality are still in abundance. If you're in denial or have found a road that has no such obstacles, chances are it's not taking you anyplace worth going. The challenge is to convert obstacles into opportunities.

The importance of shared leadership cannot be underestimated because once that goal is accomplished, many other inequities will be corrected. I am convinced that more women in decision-making posts in industry and government and other professions will lead to business practices, legislation, and a culture where all Americans can compete more fairly. Because most women have experienced unfair treatment of one kind or another, I believe we are much more likely to address inequities and, when we have the power, to fix them.

As we explore our strategy for making shared leadership a way of life, we need to remember how long women have been spectators rather than players. Changing that paradigm is the hill to be climbed—a hill with a slope that, even on our best days, must be called slippery.

Here are four obstacles. There are more, but these four will be enough to make the point that we need to be ready to overcome obstacles as we strive for change.

Obstacle One: The Math

In business, the CEO ratio of men and women is massive. In looking at the measuring stick of the Fortune 500 companies, I remember the elation we experienced when there were actually twenty-five women in the CEO jobs of top firms, and that's only 10 percent of where shared leadership should take us.

To improve the math, we must not only make significant progress against the current numbers but we also must deal with executive turnover. CEOs retire, regardless of gender. That time came for **Indra Nooyi** of PepsiCo, for **Denise Morrison** of Campbell, for **Margo Georgiadis** of Mattel, for **Sherilyn McCoy** of Avon, and for **Meg Whitman** of Hewlett-Packard.

When those women executives left, all were replaced by men. There's nothing wrong with that. No one promised that once a woman earned the corner office, she would have gender rights to it forever.

While we're celebrating getting there, we also have to concentrate on staying there, which brings us back to the math, the need to ensure that the corporate pipeline runs all the way to the top so that when the top job has a vacancy, the list of prospects includes the names of women.

The math is a little different in government. The imbalance between women and men in public office is somewhat more visible. We can count the numbers in Congress, in state legislatures, in governors' offices, and in appointed cabinet positions. The shared leadership goal of fifty-fifty is more controllable in the government. The formula is as near as the ballot box. More women running for office. More women winning.

Our assembly kit for overcoming obstacles must include family-friendly policies in the workplace that recognize a woman's unique role in the home. Motherhood or caregiving responsibilities of any kind must not impede her opportunity for promotion. In this high-tech age, we must be smart enough to understand the worth and the fairness involved in such policies. Women are valuable to their company's success. They have experience. They know what it's like to have the wind in your face, and it is a loss to us all to squander a deep pool of leadership.

Obstacle Two: The Myth

The late Congresswoman **Bella Abzug** said, "All the men on my staff can type." The irony in her comment recalls another time when it was unthinkable to imagine equal rights for women—in the classroom, in the workplace, in the justice system, and in the voting booth. Now, hopefully, the myth that perpetuated such a national attitude has faded away.

Abzug also said, "You're not going to have a society that understands its humanity if you don't have more women in government."

To eliminate the myth that women are not strong leaders, many more of us need to step over the threshold. Women with leadership potential and interest must not wait, or someone else will have closed the door on the opportunity.

So much about leadership or advancing your own ideas relates to timing. I do not profess to know whether these are the best of times or the worst of times, but we need to think of this as the only time. We can shape a future for women that will relieve new generations from the anxiety that we charitably call second place. I contend that second place is last place.

We cannot generalize about women any more than we can generalize about men. Sentences that begin with the phrase "all women" are not true. Those who try to put labels on an entire gender sometimes claim a superiority for males. That is the myth we need to erase so that equality means what it implies.

Obstacle Three: The Priorities

Massive military expenditures. Staggering amounts in political campaign contributions. Huge tax breaks for industry. I understand what's happening. I recognize the need for a first-class military to protect the freedom we all value. And the way political campaigns are now run seems to call for a choking supply of money. And, yes, our business sector propels the economic engine of the nation.

I believe that more women in position to make decisions on how our resources are allocated will opt for balance between old practices and new directions that benefit people who need a voice. Children, for example. Kids don't vote, but it will be women who make sure the young are not ignored when it comes to tax credits. Kids don't send in campaign contributions, but it will be women who insist they are not shortchanged on educational opportunities. And young people don't pay taxes, but it will be women who will pass the laws protecting them from the dangers of everyday life.

Marian Wright Edelman, one of the most candid boosters for the young, sees it this way: "Children cannot eat rhetoric, and they cannot be sheltered by commissions that study the needs of kids. It isn't complicated. They need our help." Women in business are certain to produce products that are more consumer-friendly. Women in government are certain to redirect governmental spending so that the nation's values reflect our respect for the young, the not-so-young, our military men and women, and all those suffering from health problems. And women leaders in education are certain to provide a learning experience unparalleled in American history.

Why am I so sure of this? Because consumerism, caring, and advocacy for others have dominated the lives of women. We don't regard these as women's issues. They are human issues that need to be on America's agenda.

Obstacle Four: The Mission

We have to stay focused on the mission: equality for women. Straying from it can lead to a self-constructed barrier. The happy ending we want to write to this story depends on our ability to achieve an effective unity of purpose and the use of our resources to support actions that will make a difference. Unity and money.

Unity because without it, we lose the ability to make change through collective impact. The hundreds of organizations in America that have women's rights on their agenda need to imagine how strong a united voice from a coalition that captures their message could be. We measure our ability to bring about change not by our widely distributed intentions but by our unified potential.

As for money, if women would mobilize their philanthropic muscle behind the issues of equality, the mountain would start to move. As organizations, we need to evolve and change with the needs around us. Existing simply to repeat what we did last year holds no appeal for me. Most women harbor a reluctance, even a suspicion, about joining the financial resources of their organization with those of other groups—not realizing that in lessening your own identity, you may move a lot closer to the goal you want.

Vision 2020 is an example. We created it with the clear purpose of jump-starting a national conversation on the unfinished business of women's equality. We chose to do that with a focus on the four areas of awareness I have discussed—shared leadership, economic security, youth education, and women's increased civic engagement. We set a firm timetable for the Year 2020, when we would issue a national report card on how America is doing in those four categories.

When 2020 comes, when we have filled the 366 days of that year with attention-getting information on how to finish the job that the suffragists began, then Vision 2020 will evolve into a different organization, perhaps as a national clearinghouse of information on women's progress.

Are the four areas discussed in this chapter obstacles? Or opportunities?

If someone told me today that all the Fortune 500 companies had immediate openings at the CEO level and that each of them wanted to hire a woman for that position and if they asked me, "Where can you find five hundred chief executive women for us?" I would say, "In many places." I would review the roster of thousands of women who have their own businesses and who, on a smaller scale, have already dealt with the wilderness of budgets, strategy, and marketing. I would check the availability of college presidents who have become skilled at balancing the demands of multiple constituencies. I would examine the strength of the next woman up—the women in each of the 500 companies, the ones who have shown the most promising management skills. And I would look at the amazing memberships of women's professional organizations, like the International Women's Forum, and to executive search firms, like Diversified Search, with a track record of placing top-level women.

And then, of course, I would ask men. Enlightened men. Men who not only believe women have something to offer in terms of leadership but also believe that the equality path is the right route to travel.

Those men have discovered what women already knew—that there's a certain Darwinian quality at work; meaning that those who survive and thrive are not necessarily faster or stronger, but they have an enviable adaptability to change.

CHAPTER 16

Unfinished Business

From Earhart to Jemison, from Paul to Steinem, from Amendment XIX to Title IX—the last one hundred years have been times of encouragement and challenge for the American woman. Progress makes one thing clear: there's still some unfinished business out there.

In the run-up to the midterm elections of 2018, the Pew Research Center conducted a survey about the impact of increased numbers of women running for the U.S. Congress. They concluded that while the majority of respondents say there are too few women in political office, there was little consensus among the men and women surveyed that having more women in Congress would lead to any significant change in the way Washington does its business.

I wish they had called me.

Had the Pew people called and asked me my opinion on whether more women in Congress would mean more changes in the nation's priorities, I would have said, "It depends on how many more." Give women a majority of the seats, and I believe you would see an instant emphasis on health, education, and other social legislation that affects families.

That's what happens when the majority rules.

This is not a criticism of all men. There have been some strong leaders in Washington over the years, and at times, they've been compassionate. Women don't want to take away their leadership. We just want to share it.

Since women and men share so many experiences already, why not one more—the sharing of leadership in business and in government, for starters. Sharing the risks and the rewards, the expectations and the results. When that happens, America will be that much more of a model to the world.

The reason I'm an advocate of shared leadership is that I'm convinced that having both genders at the table debating the issues, setting priorities, and allocating resources will have a much more positive outcome for all our lives and our families' lives. The unfinished business of women's equality awaits the best that men and women working together can bring to the challenge.

Here are twelve potential positive combinations that can result from shared leadership:

1. Power Tempered by Patience
   Power changes things. Patience makes sure the list includes the things that truly need changing.
2. Leadership Enriched by Loyalty
   Loyalty to purpose and principle is fundamental to the success and influence of those who lead.
3. Progress Sparked by Partnership
   Progress requires continuous curiosity about the unreasonable, the improbable, and the impossible. It works better when both men and women combine their curiosity.
4. Achievement Enabled by Action
   Earlier in this book is the story of how Febb Ensminger Burn believed the achievement of the Nineteenth Amendment was crucial and that the Tennessee Legislature must ratify it. Her son was in that legislature. She encouraged him. He cast the deciding vote. Action and achievement are lasting companions.

5. Reputation Enhanced by Respect
   An organization's reputation is the result of the way it conducts its business. Being a place that values respect among women and men is a great start.
6. Cooperation Reached by Compromise
   Cooperation takes practice, sometimes years, until it becomes one's lifestyle. Compromise doesn't mean giving up the high ground, just cultivating it differently. Keep your eye on the end goal, then reach an agreement.
7. Optimism Created by Opportunity
   Leaders who stimulate optimism by making sure opportunity is equal for all can count on a workforce that thinks there's nothing so good that it can't get better.
8. Victory Accelerated by Vision
   Knowing what the ideal looks like before you start to build it—that is the worth of vision. Communicating it to others can lead to victory.
9. Competition Stimulated by Creativity
   In a climate of equality, all will be measured by what their brainpower brings to attaining a goal. Generating that climate is what leaders do through motivation and managing.
10. Rewards Earned by Results
    Nothing makes people more confident in their leader than the sharing of recognition for a success. It might be money or praise or promotion. Whatever form it takes, people need to know that the applause is fairly distributed.
11. Excellence Inspired by Enthusiasm
    A part of creating the kind of environment champions want is to realize not everybody on the team is used to being a winner. Many women have gone through life being taught to be in awe of the strength and competence of others. Encouragement is in order.

12. Success Shaped by Sharing
    Sometimes the line is very thin between who gets to make decisions and who doesn't, between those who feel they are an important part of the task and those who feel they are on the outside looking in. Women like to compete as much as men, and a real leader will see that the arena is open to them.

Does the adoption of a policy of equality for women assure a near-perfect workplace with the dozen positive conditions just reviewed? In matters of human relationships, there are no money-back guarantees, but several things are almost certain to occur.

- Women will no longer be paid less than men for the same work.
- Women will know they have the same opportunity for promotion as men do.
- Women will be included in discussions of strategies, policies, and practices.
- A higher level of team productivity will emerge.

Well over half a century ago, Great Britain's Roger Bannister did what many said could not be done by the human body. He ran a mile in under four minutes. Once the barrier was broken, other athletes promptly took another twelve seconds and more off the record. Believing that women's equality is not only the right thing to do but that it is also best for an organization should be incentive enough to take the necessary steps to correct conditions that have been uneven from the beginning.

Shared leadership is not so much about achieving a personal best. It is about accomplishing a team best. There's something special about the concept of unity, of women and men working together to reach a goal. That's only possible when a sense of equality exists.

It does not take any particular genius to recognize that America continues to be a land of contrasts, of imbalances that are sometimes baffling. In a robust economy with hundreds of thousands of unfilled jobs, we have hundreds of thousands of unemployed people. In a nation with seventeen thousand libraries, one hundred thousand schools, and over three million teachers, we still have too many people who can neither read nor write. And then there's the imbalance that is particularly troubling. We live in a wonderful country that produces so much food we pay farmers not to produce it, while nearly forty million Americans are uncertain where their next meal is coming from.

One thing we don't have a surplus of is leaders. We need more take-charge people who see problems and solve them, more people willing to fulfill their public service instincts. My travels and work for women's rights have allowed me to observe women from all fifty states—women who are both workplace leaders and positive examples of civic engagement.

I cannot close this case for shared leadership, for women and men working together as leaders, without remembering Olympic Champion **Jackie Joyner-Kersee**. In 1988, in Seoul, South Korea, she competed in the heptathlon—seven events to determine the best all-around athlete. In competition with women from all over the world, she won four of the seven events and finished strong enough in the other three to post a world record that still stands.

As she displayed her gold medal on many occasions thereafter, she praised her coach, who was her husband, saying, "We won it together." That's shared leadership.

CHAPTER 17

Rules for the Majority

We know what women can achieve. We know how a majority can change things. The characteristics that follow are reminders of what's needed in order for us to *think* like the majority we are.

Majority Rule 1: Confidence

One of the most underestimated joys of life is learning to live in peace with yourself. Do we have a plan for that, or do we just make it up as we go along? Can we understand that if we are ever to act like the majority we are, we need a lifetime supply of self-esteem? Consider the words of **Eleanor Roosevelt**: "No one can make you feel inferior without your consent."

Majority Rule 2: Resilience

In 1848, the first Women's Rights Convention got it right in its Declaration of Sentiments and Resolutions: "We hold these truths to be self-evident: that all men <u>and women</u> are created equal." It's not necessary to look outside yourself for assurance that equality is a reality. Your behavior can export that freedom to those around you.

Majority Rule 3: Hope

Hope helps us see a future filled with the equality we want. Working toward that goal is even better as you know that you are one of those people who can convert your dreams to reality. The will precedes the way.

Majority Rule 4: Participation

Suffragist Carrie Chapman Catt said it this way: "The vote is a power, a weapon of offense and defense, a prayer ... Two generations of women have given their lives and their fortunes to secure the vote ... No man in our own or any other country has sacrificed one-tenth as much for the vote."

Majority Rule 5: Respect

Vision 2020 honors the past because the women of another time laid the groundwork that challenges us to take their battle to a successful conclusion. They did what they did in a storm and, in doing so, left us with a relative calm, which we must use with remembrance and resolve to complete that unfinished business of women's equality.

Majority Rule 6: Perseverance

Competitive athletes know that you can't win without persevering. If we pause to enjoy for just a moment the progress we've made, that's OK. But when the moment is over, let's realize there are still doors to be opened for women. We should no longer doubt our ability to claim a final victory.

Majority Rule 7: Belief

No women can fly on a combat mission, World War II photographer **Margaret Bourke-White** was told. She asked, "Why not?" She took photos of bombers and photographed world leaders, concentration camps, and even the torpedoed ship she was on. The question is, What else is it they say we can't do?

Majority Rule 8: Discontent

It's useful to remind ourselves of the phrase "You get what you settle for" as a caution against complacency. I've got a job, a wonderful family, and some money in the bank. But it's not time to be content. Still on our collective to-do list are shared leadership, economic security, and civic engagement. It's not a time to ease up on the gas pedal just yet.

Majority Rule 9: Competitive Spirit

Most people I know like a challenge, but not necessarily a winner-loser outcome. Achieving gender equality and shared leadership should be a win-win.

Majority Rule 10: Boldness

Zora Neale Hurston recalled that her mother urged her at every opportunity to "jump at the sun," saying, "You might not land on the sun, but at least you'll get off the ground." Action is the essential companion of ambition. By doing something, you can get a better view of what remains to be done. Fear merely lessens the time available to get it done.

Majority Rule 11: Independence

In addition to all those years without the vote, an injustice was the historical imposition of economic dependence on women. Women couldn't own property or get credit in their own names and had limited opportunities to demonstrate that they could run a business, govern a state, and command a spacecraft. We must ensure that the twenty-first Century has ended the era of limited opportunities for women.

Majority Rule 12: The Will to Change

One revolution never quite looks like another. They come in all sizes and shapes. Voices can rally unity. Unity can increase the volume, making sure those in power develop a better sense of hearing. Change cannot be far behind.

Majority Rule 13: Optimism

The work ahead is to ensure that generations of women who follow us can walk into futures filled with choices.

Majority Rule 14: Risk-Taking

The limbs we crawl out on can become bridges to the equality we seek. The walls we climb without knowing what is on the other side can be stepping-stones to a more fulfilling life. The crawling and climbing can be classified as risks or as adventures. Late-in-life regrets are often not about things we did but rather about the things we never tried.

Majority Rule 15: Action

Questions like "Where will you be ten years from now?" never held any appeal for me. Life is filled with so many unexpected turns in the road—all of which can be translated into opportunities—that predicting where you will be only slows you down from getting there. Have a dream, yes! But entertain the probability that the path to that dream is straight ahead. The journey can be even better than the destination.

Majority Rule 16: Inspiration

It's a good idea to learn more about yourself. When you do, you may find out that you have more power than you thought, more courage than you require, and more time than you imagined to do the things that will make you your own role model. Create your own inspiration.

Majority Rule 17: Communication

Vision 2020's optimism about a new dimension of partnership among women and men is based on confidence that the era of sharing has arrived. No longer unresponsive to the concept of women as leaders, many men are making adjustments. While the two genders may speak slightly different languages, both will become more fluent in understanding equality.

Majority Rule 18: Readiness for a Challenge

Memories are special, but we can't afford to have them outnumber our dreams. Shaping the future is a challenge that demands a more exciting preview of coming attractions than anything that has happened for women until now.

Majority Rule 19: Inclusiveness

If we are to achieve a lasting equality for women where each of us can succeed or fail on our own merits, then a much greater sense of unity must be attained. We have too many individuals and too many organizations competing with one another for those "crumbs of power" protecting their own turf and not working together.

Majority Rule 20: Leadership

There is a certain dignity that comes with being a leader. Integrity accompanies you in every decision. You won't have to look far to find expectations. You have them of yourself. Others have them of you. Whatever motivates you—the goal, the doubters, or a distant drum—rely on it to supply the emotional energy to pursue your purpose.

And Finally ...

We honor the past because we cannot live there with any illusion of changing what happened. We cheer it because it's our foundation for learning what brave women did under severe restrictions. We need not try to escape the past, but we must not become stuck in it. It's over. Its value as a guide continues.

We enrich the present because it's where we live. Here is where we get to showcase our willingness to exercise responsibility. It is now that we can advocate for women's equality, encourage women's increased civic engagement, and speak up for economic parity. Time moves at an unforgiving pace. If we don't use it, it will use us.

We shape the future because we are determined to intercept the pattern of generations of girls growing up with limited options. Women have so much to bring to a world that is still in search of peace, is still in need of respect, and is still in hope of building what **Maya Angelou** calls "a future plump with promise."

We women—the majority—can show the way. Make that *must* show the way. After all, Majority Rules.

APPENDIX

LETTER TO MAE YEAKEL AND CHLOE ARIAS

Dear Mae and Chloe,

When I came to the section of this book about shaping the future, you both came immediately to my mind. I watched with pride as you grew up. I marveled with awe at how fast the years flew by as you went off to college. I thrilled at the thought that in 2020, you will both vote in your first presidential election.

I used to say that the work I was doing for women's equality was to make things better for a time I would not see. I was wrong. In you and so many other young women in your generation, I am already seeing character and commitment that will carry this campaign for women's equality to the heights we envision.

I invite you—yes, urge you—and all young women to learn from the pioneering spirit of the suffragists and the unflinching courage of so many women who have come before you and then get on with shaping a future that, once and for all time, defines equality.

With anticipation, from your grandmother,

Lynn Hardy Yeakel

Vision 2020
EQUALITY IN SIGHT®

Vision 2020 is a national women's equality coalition representing over 22 million people, including women leaders from coast to coast. Headquartered at Drexel University's Institute for Women's Health and Leadership in Philadelphia, the coalition is made up of more than one hundred national and regional organizations working to achieve economic, political, and social equality for women.

Through their Delegates and Allied Organizations from across the United States, VISION 2020 seeks to accelerate the pace of women's progress. Individuals align themselves with VISION 2020 as they work to achieve and promote gender equality. Allied Organizations receive support for their initiatives as the coalition builds awareness for their work. This mutually beneficial relationship leverages collective impact to complete the unfinished business of women's equality.

The VISION 2020 Mission focuses on four pillars of action:

Shared Leadership
Youth Education
Economic Parity
Civic Engagement

Throughout each year, VISION 2020 hosts programs and events to elevate these pillars.

A pinnacle for VISION 2020 is the centennial of the Nineteenth Amendment, marking one hundred years of women's right to vote. In the year 2020, the coalition commemorates this historical event and also assesses the present-day status of women in relation to shared leadership, economic parity, and civic engagement through its yearlong Women 100 celebration (see women100.org).

Go to drexel.edu/vision2020.

ABOUT THE AUTHOR

Lynn H. Yeakel is Director of Drexel University College of Medicine's Institute for Women's Health and Leadership, where she holds the Betty A. Cohen Chair in Women's Health. Yeakel is the Founder and President of Vision 2020, a national initiative of the Institute to achieve women's economic, political, and social equality.

A coalition of more than one hundred national and regional organizations representing over 22 million people and women leaders who are Delegates from coast to coast, Vision 2020 launched an American Conversation about Women and Leadership in 2010. Vision 2020's objectives include achieving fifty-fifty shared leadership among women and men in business and government and increasing women's civic engagement.

Yeakel was a founder of Women's Way, the first and largest women's fundraising coalition in the nation and served as its CEO from 1980 until 1992, when she ran for the U.S. Senate. She drew national attention in what was called the Year of the Woman, winning the primary and nearly unseating the longtime incumbent.

Yeakel is a Phi Beta Kappa graduate and former trustee of Randolph-Macon Woman's College and received a Master of Science in Management degree from the American College. She has long been active in leadership positions for local and national nonprofit organizations and is the recipient of numerous honors and awards.

Her first book, *A Will and a Way* (2010), presents insights into the key issues of women's independence based on her own experience and lessons from history.

INDEX

A

Abzug, Bella, 92
Adams, Abigail, 20, 36
Albright, Madeleine, 58
American Woman Suffrage Association, 12
Anthony, Susan B., 2–3, 20, 38

B

Bannister, Roger, 99
Barra, Mary, xiv, 50
barriers, 9
  overcoming, 11
Bethane-Cookman University, 16–17
Bethune, Mary McLeod, 16–17
Blakwell, Alice Stone, 5
Bourke-White, Margaret, 103
Brennan, Megan, 55
Brittain, Deborah, 84
Buck, Pearl, 9
Bumpers, Betty, 57
Burn, Febb Ensminger, 27–28, 32, 97
Burn, Harry, letter to, 32
Burn, J. T.. See Burn, Febb Ensminger
Bush, George H. W., 24
Butler, Susan, 84–85

C

Carville, James, 63
Catt, Carrie Chapman, 3, 33, 35, 102
change, xiii, xvi, 10, 32, 82, 104
  resistance to, 5
Chisholm, Shirley, 64, 67
Clinton, Hillary, 58

Cohen, Walter, 74

D

Daytona Normal and Industrial Institute, 17
democracy, 39, 44, 82
Dock, Lavinia Lloyd, 4
Duniway, Abigail Jane Scott, 2–3
Dunwoody, Ann, xii
D. Walter Cohen Shared Leadership Scholarship, 74
Dykstra, Candy, 6

E

Earhart, Amelia, 9, 19, 47
Edelman, Marian Wright, 44, 93
education, youth, xiv, 51
Eighteenth Amendment, 47, 70
Eisner, Jane, 79
engagement, civic, xiv, 51, 64, 85, 100
equality, 39, 44, 48, 51, 77, 81, 98
  look of, 83

F

Fairgrave, Phoebe, 9
Faust, Drew Gilpin, 55
Field, Sara Bard, 4
Fitzgerald, Ella, 14–15
freedom, 65
French, Lizzie Crozier, 34
Friedan, Betty, 8
Fry, John, 71

G

Georgiadis, Margo, 91
Gibson, Althea, 18
Greco, Rosemarie, 89–90
Green, Edith, 72
Guthrie, Janet, 47

H

Haley, Nikki, 55
Harper, Ida, 47
Harris, Mary, 6
Higgins, Katie, xiv
Hill, Anita, 24–26, 59
Hobby, Oveta Culp, 15–17
Howard, Michelle, xiv, 55
Hurston, Zora Neale, 47, 103
Hutton, Edward Francis, 52

J

Jordan, Barbara, 10, 67
Jordan, Michael, 50
Joyner-Kersee, Jackie, 100

K

Kennedy, John F., 66
King, Billie Jean, 6

L

labor, 55
Lamar, Hedy, 6
leadership, xi, 8, 56, 73, 92, 106
  shared, xii, 37, 50–52, 67, 74, 77, 86, 90, 97, 99–100
Ledbetter, Lilly, 53–54
Leslie, Frank, 38
Leslie, Miriam, 37
Lincoln, Abraham, xi, 55
Lindbergh, Anne Morrow, 67

M

majority, rules for, 106
Mary Bethune, 16
McCoy, Sherilyn, 91
Meir, Golda, 50
Meriwether, Elizabeth Avery, 34
Milton, Abby Crawford, 33
Mink, Patsy, 72
Mitchell, Jackie, 6
Morrison, Denise, 91
Mother Jones. See Harris, Mary
Mott, Lucretia, 8, 36–37, 44

N

Napravnik, Rosie, 24
National American Woman Suffrage Association, 12, 35
National Woman Suffrage Association, 11
Newell, Emily Jane, 3
Nineteenth Amendment, 5, 10, 28, 31–32, 44
Niota, lady from. See Burn, Febb Ensminger
Nooyi, Indra, 91

O

obstacles, 56, 90–95
Ocasio-Cortez, Alexandria, 67
Olson, Kimberly, 86–87
Overall, Frances Holder, 34

P

parity, economic, xiii, 51, 53–54
Parks, Rosa, xii
Paul, Alice, 2–4, 38–39
Pelosi, Nancy, 58
people, kinds of, 71
Pesotta, Rose, 17–18
Pew Research Center, 96

Post, Marjorie Merriweather, 52
present, enriching the, 71–74
progress, xvi, 20, 96–97
Putnam, George, 47

R

Rankin, Jeannette, 11
respect, xv, 102
Rice, Condoleezza, 58
Roberts, Barbara, 85–86
Robinson, Lori, 24
Roosevelt, Eleanor, 17, 37, 45, 101
Roosevelt, Franklin D., xi, 9, 23
Ross, Nellie, 21–23
Ross, William, 22
Rowe, Charlotte, 37

S

Sandler, Bernice, 71–73
Shalala, Donna, 59
Shaw, Anna Howard, 3
Sherman, Janann, 29
Sojourner Truth, 8
Sotomayor, Sonia, xii
Specter, Arlen, 11, 25
Stanton, Elizabeth Cady, 2, 8, 11, 20–21, 37, 44–45
Stofan, Ellen, 19, 50
Stone, Lucy, 12
suffragists, 10, 12, 29
Summit, Pat, 27, 59

T

Tayloe, Nellie Davis. *See* Ross, Nellie
Taylor, Lucy, 6
tenacity, 46–47
Terrell, Mary Eliza Church, 30–31
Terrell philosophy, 31
Thomas, Clarence, 24
Title IX, 44, 71–72, 74
Toast to Tenacity, 46, 70

Twenty-First Amendment, 70

V

Vaught, Wilma, 11
Vision 2020, 15, 34, 46, 67, 69–71, 77, 87, 94, 95, 102, 105
 agenda of, 80
 congresses of, 80–81, 83
 Declaration of Equality, 48, 81
 focus of, xvii
 goals of, 51, 68
 voting, 1, 10, 21, 65, 69

W

Warner, Kate Burch, 34
Wells, Marguerite Milton, 3
White, Mettie, 33
Whitman, Meg, 91
Williams, Charl Ormond, 34
Wilson, Woodrow, 4, 38
Wolf, Tom, 70
Woman One, 74
Women 100, 68, 81
Women's Auxiliary Army Corps, 16
Women's History Month, xiv–xv
Women's Rights Convention, 2, 21, 37, 101

Y

Yellen, Janet, xiv
Yellin, Carol Lynn, 29
Young, Peggy, 54